P9-APW-982

Church and Campus

Church and Campus

Legal Issues in Religiously Affiliated Higher Education

Philip R. Moots and
Edward McGlynn Gaffney, Jr.

UNIVERSITY OF NOTRE DAME PRESS
NOTRE DAME LONDON

Library of Congress Cataloging in Publication Data

Moots, Philip R
Church and campus.

Includes bibliographical references.
1. Church colleges—Law and legislation—United States. I. Gaffney, Edward McGlynn, joint author. II. Title.
KF4124.M6 344'.73'074 79-14002
ISBN 0-268-00731-4
ISBN 0-268-00732-2 pbk.

Manufactured in the United States of America

Contents

Appendices

Foreword

WE ARE BY NOW too painfully aware of the dramatic increase in legal problems which have risen to confront colleges and universities in the past decade or so, problems ranging from a sharp expansion of government regulation to the general kinds of legal issues presented by an increasingly litigious society. Those legal issues have been particularly challenging for independent and religiously affiliated institutions of higher learning. It was in response to their problems that Notre Dame established the Center for Constitutional Studies in its Law School in August 1977. Its primary purpose is to provide basic legal scholarship and selected advocacy activities in issues affecting independent and religiously affiliated colleges and universities.

This study is the first of what we hope will be a continuing series of studies from the Center to assist administrators and attorneys of colleges and religious bodies, national educational executives, the courts, and legislators across the nation in meeting these enormously complex legal issues. I believe this publication is an incisive and important first step in that process, and I am pleased that the University of Notre Dame in cooperation with the Association of Catholic Colleges and Universities is able to offer a scholarly contribution to this important task.

(Rev.) Theodore M. Hesburgh, C.S.C.
President
University of Notre Dame

Preface

THE PUBLICATION OF THIS STUDY is the welcome outcome of a project of several years standing.

An Ad Hoc Committee of civil and canon (church) lawyers was set up in the Association of Catholic Colleges and Universities to investigate issues of property ownership and control affecting church-related colleges and the religious bodies which are somehow related to them.

Several factors suggested the need for the study. First, colleges which formerly were organized as a part of a single parent corporation, i.e., the sponsoring religious institute or congregation, have recently been established as separate corporate entities. Second, this development was accompanied by the introduction of many laypersons to boards of trustees which had typically been composed only (or mostly) of members of religious orders or congregations. Third, with the emergence of federal and state programs of aid to higher education, eligibility for participation in these programs depended upon institutions passing constitutional tests spelled out in various court opinions in the last decade. Finally, differing opinions had arisen about how to guard the assets and maintain the religious goals and integrity of church-related colleges.

The Ad Hoc Committee was chaired by Rev. James Coriden, Dean of the Washington Theological Union. Other members were Dean John Garvey of the Columbus School of Law of the Catholic University of America, Rev. Frederick R. McManus, vice provost and dean of graduate studies at Catholic University, Rev. Ladislas Orsy, S.J., professor of canon law at Catholic University, and Rev. Charles Whelan, S.J., professor of law in the Fordham University School of Law.

As the Committee began to sketch its plans for the study, the members raised other questions which they felt should be of equal concern to the colleges and their sponsors. In particular, they expressed concern over the potential liability of the sponsoring religious bodies for the actions or alleged negligence of their colleges and over the ability of church-related colleges to exercise religious preference in faculty and staff hiring and in student admissions.

Since the Committee was made up of full-time teachers and administrators, the expanded scope of the study seemed ready to threaten the project. Fortunately, just at that time the University of Notre Dame founded the Center for Constitutional Studies in its Law School and engaged Mr. Philip R. Moots as Director and Mr. Edward McGlynn Gaffney, Jr., as Associate Director. Because Mr. Moots had served as special counsel to the Board of Higher Education and Ministry of the United Methodist Church, he was familiar with the issues the Committee was raising and had a special interest in them. Mr. Moots and Mr. Gaffney accepted responsibility for the extensive legal research and writing for the project. We appreciate the thoughtful analysis which they have provided.

Two other elements in the history of this project should be mentioned. First, very helpful suggestions were offered in the course of the study by a number of representatives of church-related colleges affiliated with other denominations. It was quickly evident that concerns in these areas were shared across denominational lines. Second, the project received a small grant from the AGB Studies Program of the Association of Governing Boards. We are grateful for these suggestions and this support.

A first draft of this study was presented to participants in three seminars sponsored by the ACCU. Held in New York and Chicago in November, 1978, and in Washington in February, 1979, they brought together college administrators, church body representatives, and legal counsel whose wisdom and experience were put to work on the issues presented. I mention this because of the added value in having the questions and the conclusions "road-tested" by the users themselves.

A note about the appendices: at an early stage, it was thought to combine questions of church discipline with those of civil law. However, this plan was altered somewhat in order to provide the civil law matters in an uninterrupted fashion, reserving to the appendices briefer comments about requirements of the various church communions. It may be that denominational groups will wish to pursue these questions separately, as they do not always lend themselves to a common effort.

Both denominational leaders and administrators at religiously affiliated colleges have a vital interest in the integrity of church-related higher education in America. We hope that this study will serve as useful guidance in the resolution of some of the difficult legal questions facing these colleges and will stimulate further discussion of these important issues.

Msgr. John F. Murphy
Executive Director
Association of Catholic Colleges
and Universities

Acknowledgments

IN 1977 THE UNIVERSITY OF NOTRE DAME established the Center for Constitutional Studies at the Notre Dame Law School to engage in scholarly research and analysis concerning legal problems encountered by independent and religiously affiliated institutions of higher education. The authors of this study are the professional staff of the Center. We wish to express our appreciation to the University for its continuing financial support for the work of the Center.

As Monsignor Murphy indicates in the Preface, this study was sponsored by the Association of Catholic Colleges and Universities, which initiated the project, organized seminars to discuss the themes presented here, and provided a subsidy to support the publication of this volume. We are deeply grateful to Monsignor Murphy for his leadership in this project and to all of the members of the ACCU committee mentioned in the Preface, who have given us the benefit of their comments on the first draft of the manuscript. In addition, Father Charles Whalen assisted Mr. Moots in giving presentations and leading the discussion at two of the seminars sponsored by the ACCU. Father Coriden and Father McManus prepared a comment (Appendix A) on the present status of Roman Catholic canon law related to some of the matters discussed in this volume.

We also had the benefit of comments on the first draft from a broadly ecumenical group of executives of denominationally based associations of higher education, for which we are also grateful. We are especially grateful to the leadership of the United Methodist Church and the Southern Baptist Convention for authorizing and subsidizing two reports included as appendices in this volume. These two denominations have remained deeply committed to higher education as an integral mission of the church. The analysis of their experiences in this area provided by two thoughtful attorneys, Kent M. Weeks and Preston H. Callison, should be of interest and value to all church groups engaged in higher education.

The chairman of the Center's advisory board, the Rev. James T. Burtchaell, C.S.C., and our colleague at Notre Dame Law School Professor Robert E. Rodes, Jr., also reviewed the manuscript and offered comments which invariably helped to improve the document. We acknowledge this assistance gratefully, and we tender to them and to all the readers of the manuscript the customary absolution of responsibility for the final version of the text.

Responsibility for drafting and editing this document was shared by the authors. Philip R. Moots had primary responsibility for preparing the Introduction and chapters one through three and seven through nine. Edward McGlynn Gaffney, Jr., had primary responsibility for the remaining chapters. Both authors reviewed one another's drafts and provided critical comments.

The following interns associated with the Center provided valuable research undergirding the legal analysis contained in this study: Mrs. Ethna Bennert Cooper, Ms. Gracia Bollerud, Mr. Raymond Dalton, Miss Barbara Kramer, Sister Kathleen Moroney, C.S.C., and Mr. John Selent.

We wish to express special thanks to our Administrative Assistant, Mrs. Rosemary Reiter, who has generously labored long hours, often overtime, to produce the typescript of this study. She has not only been extremely competent but unfailingly gracious under the pressure of meeting deadlines.

Finally, we are grateful to Mr. James Langford, Director of the University of Notre Dame Press, and to Ms. Ann Rice,

Executive Editor of the Press, for their marvelous editorial assistance and willingness to publish this volume within a brief space of time.

We hope that this volume will be of service to everyone interested in preserving the integrity and autonomy of religiously affiliated higher education in this country.

Philip R. Moots
Edward McGlynn Gaffney, Jr.,
Center for Constitutional Studies
Notre Dame Law School
April, 1979

Introduction

IN RECENT YEARS there has been a remarkable number of studies and publications by religious denominations engaged in higher education reflecting upon their experiences in this endeavor and considering likely directions for the future.[1] Among the issues examined in these studies are fundamental questions of why churches and other religious bodies are engaged in higher education and what kinds of influence they can and should exercise in the life of the campus consistent with academic freedom and the basic mission of the college or university.

A multitude of legal issues emerge from these deliberations and the experiences of religiously affiliated colleges in this nation. Among the most important are the following: a) the imposition of legal liability ("ascending liability") upon the religious body as a result of actions of the college, b) the eligibility of religiously affiliated colleges and their students for public financial assistance, c) legal questions raised by government regulations which are uniquely applicable to religiously affiliated colleges, and d) property ownership and control questions.

It has been widely observed that there has been an "explosive burst" in the resort to litigation of all kinds in this nation,[2] including a particularly sharp increase in government regulation, a situation of great concern to higher education.[3] Other nonprofit institutions related to religious bodies in this nation, such as hospitals, homes for the elderly, and other educational and vocational institutions, also face burgeoning legal problems.[4] In many instances, the issues discussed here overlap with those of concern to other church related institutions. This study, however, will focus exclusively on higher education and will not explore in depth the points of similarity and difference between colleges and other nonprofit institutions.[5]

Current legal trends underline the importance for leaders of colleges and of religious bodies to establish legal guidelines and reference points in defining the relationships with each other. There is obviously considerable difficulty in discussing universally applicable guidelines, given the enormous diversity of patterns of relationships among various religious bodies and the colleges to which they relate in this country. In some instances, of course, the religious body owns the campus and its property, and controls in every sense its governance mechanisms. In other instances the relationship between the two institutions is important to both, but the campus is entirely autonomous in governance and ownership. In still other instances, there may be formal elements of ownership and legal control by the religious body which have become nearly meaningless in operation. The variations are almost endless.[6]

It is the goal of this study, in terms sufficiently general to be useful to as many participants in this arena as possible, to identify legal issues to be considered and steps to be taken to establish relationships which both sponsoring religious bodies and colleges agree are desirable.

We use the term "religious body" to include churches, religious orders, or church judicatories of any kind. It is our assumption that the identity of the religious body (whether a church judicatory, religious institute or congregation, or other agency of a denomination) makes little if any difference for purposes of this analysis. The terms "affiliated," "related," or "sponsoring" are used interchangeably to refer to any kind of relationship between the college and the religious body. As demonstrated elsewhere,[7] there is no single definition of what is a "church related" or a "religiously sponsored," a "Methodist" or a "Lutheran" college. Those terms have different implications depending on the underlying realities of the relationship and the kinds of legal questions presented. As we shall see, for example, a different analysis must be undertaken if the question is the constitutionality of public financing to a religiously affiliated institution rather than a question regarding the assessment of liability to a religious body for the action of a related college.

In order to keep a proper perspective on these problems, it is necessary to state the obvious: legal issues are only one aspect of the total network of relationships between a particular college and religious body. Legal issues are often given undue priority in policy discussions or even used as excuses to avoid facing the real policy issues. It cannot be emphasized too strongly that decisions cannot be made on the basis of legal considerations in isolation.

The particular legal questions treated in this study were selected because they appeared to the authors to be the most critical, prominent, and difficult questions facing church related higher education. At the same time, throughout the study we shall allude to other questions which are not discussed in detail herein. It is our assumption that as in other areas of the law, the focus of attention will be constantly shifting. What is essential is the understanding that these are serious problems which deserve attention and demand a commitment to develop means by which they can be met.

I Legal and Structural Relationships

SIGNIFICANT LEGAL QUESTIONS emerge from implications of the basic structural relationships between colleges and the religious bodies related to them, so we will begin with those issues. As a preface to that discussion, however, it is important to establish an understanding about what those structural relationships mean.

In establishing a relationship or evaluating an existing relationship, administrators of colleges and religious bodies must agree about the basic purposes which spawned their connection. Presumably these purposes include a shared sense of what is special about church related higher education and some agreement about the common mission of the institutions. Those common commitments and what they mean in terms of a relationship are expressed in a variety of ways, among them the formal legal, or what we will call "structural," bonds which link the two institutions.

Quite often discussions about the shared goals and programs of religious body and college, or even the conflicts between them, focus upon these legal or structural elements, all too frequently missing the mark. It must be emphasized at the outset that the importance of these formal elements of the relationship must be measured in the context of what is invariably a more meaningful component in determining what happens in the real-life, day-to-day operations of the campus—the administrative and faculty leadership on the campus.

It is true that in an important sense the influence or "control" which may be exercised by a religious body at a college is dependent upon who has the legal power to do what.[1] However, legal relationships are often important only insofar as they represent the exercise of power or limitation on its exercise in time of crisis or fundamental disagreement between the institutions. The commitments and motivations of the persons who establish and carry out administrative and academic policies at the institutions are far more important in determining the actual daily influence of the sponsoring religious body.

On one level this is so obvious it hardly deserves mention. However, it is the fundamental backdrop for everything which is said in this study. For example, even though the board of trustees has the responsibility of establishing the basic thrust of what happens on a campus and hiring the chief administrators who make it happen, the mere fact that a religious body has the ability to select a majority of the board has little real significance if the persons chosen by the sponsoring religious body to serve on the board do not share commitments about the institution with those who chose them. The selection process may be handled with carelessness or indifference by those responsible in the sponsoring religious body or, once the trustees have been selected, there may be little or no contact with them, thus impeding a continuing sense of direction for their considerations on campus policy matters. If divorced from shared commitments and continuing dialogue, these structural or legal relationships can be little more than bargaining chips to be used along with others by the religious body in time of crisis, when it becomes apparent (as it sometimes does) that the two institutions do not share a common sense of mission or purpose.

It is also true that, like nuclear deterrents, existing legal powers may not readily be used. Even if the related religious body holds the legal ability to compel a certain course of action by the college, there are powerful forces, both formal and informal, which may qualify or negate that power. The influence of an accrediting agency or governmental body, the views of faculty, students, or a class of influential donors, the probability of adverse publicity in the local community or within a certain constituency, threat of AAUP censure, the cost and delay of lawsuits, and a multitude of other constantly changing factors may preclude the exercise of actual legal power held by a sponsoring religious body.

In short, the legal or formal relationships between a sponsoring religious body and college should be the product of a mutual continuing commitment, rather than evidence of a historical relationship which may lose its meaning over the years.[2] Legal relationships are only a part, perhaps not even a major part, of the complex combination of elements which affect basic decisions both by religious body and related college. However, because those structural relationships do express the legal power relationship between the institutions, they deserve careful consideration.

The fact that a legal relationship exists between a religious body and a college does provide the opportunity for the religious body to exercise influence on or even control of policy decisions made by the college. The following are examples of common forms of structural relationship:

1. *Governing Documents*—Right of the sponsoring religious body to amend or control amendments to articles of incorporation and bylaws.
2. *Governing Board*—Right of the religious body to elect, nominate, veto or otherwise select all or some portion of the governing board. A related device is the requirement that all or some portion of the governing board be members of the religious body.
3. *Principal Officers*—Requirement that the president or other key officers of the college be selected by or subject to the veto of the religious body or be a member thereof.
4. *Budget; Assets*—Requirement that a religious body approve or have the right to veto some or all of the capital

or operating budget or the disposition of certain assets of the college.

Taken together, the power to control the governing documents and the composition of the governing board of a college is the power to exercise considerable influence and control over what happens at a campus. These powers must be combined, however, to insure such continuing control. If they are not, a college governing board may simply erase existing structural links at any time by amending the necessary documents.[3]

A further limitation on the exercise of control by a religious body through the governing board is that directors are frequently elected for a term of years with little or no provision for recall by the electing body. That means, of course, that if during that term the relationship of the religious body with the directors is limited, there may be no way actually to influence what the directors do with respect to any given decision, be it fundamental or peripheral to the life of the college.

It would ordinarily be possible under most state laws to design a corporate structure which would permit the overriding or reversal of an existing board of directors of the college if their decisions did not meet the approval of the sponsoring religious body. This might be accomplished by relatively straightforward removal and substitution provisions,[4] or a more subtle device such as a provision which would permit the religious body to add a sufficient number of directors at any time to take over control of the board.

The often-used requirement that a certain number of directors or principal officers be members of a particular religious body provides no continuing legal control at all, in and of itself. So long as the directors or officers meet the membership requirement, they can make any decisions they wish. Again, only the exercise of personal influence makes this provision useful as a practical matter to a related religious body.

In the event that the influence of a sponsoring religious body upon the college leadership is insufficient to direct its judgments with respect to matters such as budget allocation or disposition of assets, the requirement that these actions be taken only with the approval of the religious body is an important restraint device. Another way of arranging this element of control is the use of a double-tiered governing structure which allows the retention of selected fundamental decisions by a sponsoring religious body and permits all other actions to be taken by the board of the college. Still another device is the membership corporation which permits a religious body to exercise its reserved powers within the corporate structure of the college.[5]

Without further belaboring the point, the practical importance of the fundamental power to elect the governing board or to assert other formal, legal authority depends in significant measure upon the informal personal relationships which a related religious body has with leaders of the college. And the exercise of legal authority raises questions of legal responsibility both for institutions and individuals.

2 Liability Issues

UNDER CERTAIN CONDITIONS, legal liability may be imposed upon a religious body related to a college as a result of actions or omissions of the college and its representatives, including the trustees representing the religious body.

In light of what appear to be emerging trends of litigation involving independent colleges and universities, liability issues are likely to become increasingly urgent problems.[1] Among the factors contributing to this trend are a) the general increase in the resort to litigation in this nation,[2] b) the erosion of the charitable immunity doctrines of the various states,[3] c) the success of some plaintiffs suing independent institutions of higher education in persuading courts to find "state action" in college activities and thus imposing constitutional requirements upon those activities,[4] d) the proposals by legal scholars in recent years of additional theories to support claims of plaintiffs against independent colleges which do not require a finding of "state action,"[5] e) the interest of plaintiffs in asserting liability against the trustees of nonprofit institutions, including independent colleges, based on their fiduciary responsibilities,[6] and f) the very fact that independent colleges are under financial pressures and are forced to retrench, which contributes to the filing of suits by plaintiffs based upon contractual obligations of the colleges which they are unable to meet. Those obligations might include contracts with faculty and other employees or with suppliers or any other agency with which the college has made agreement to purchase or provide products or services.[7]

While there is a flood of cases which present new and troublesome questions about liability of the colleges themselves, there are only a few cases which directly raise issues of "ascending liability," i.e., the legal responsibility which may be attributed to religious bodies related to colleges as a result of actions of the college and its representatives. But such cases suggest serious consequences which sponsoring religious bodies must take into account. In one recent case, for example, a female student sued the college, all individual trustees, and the sponsoring religious body for damages suffered as a result of injuries she allegedly sustained from an assault in her dormitory.[8]

Ascending liability problems have also confronted other educational institutions and sponsoring religious bodies. In one such instance, individual trustees and administrators of a Jesuit high school were joined as defendants with several religious bodies which were alleged by the plaintiff to have joined together in an unlawful conspiracy in committing negligent and fraudulent acts that led to the financial collapse of the school.[9]

The magnitude of such legal problems, in terms of both the enormous potential liability of the institutions involved, and the staggering expenditures that may be required merely to defend such litigation, is underscored by lawsuits involving other institutions related to religious bodies. The widely publicized "Pacific Homes" litigation, for example, involves a class action suit by residents of retirement homes in California who named as defendants the United Methodist Church, two annual conferences, and various boards and agencies of that church.[10] The damages sought by plaintiffs exceeded $260 million, and the legal expenses incurred by various boards and agencies of the United Methodist Church in defending against that suit have reached $900,000[11] in less than two years of litigation!

While it is not possible to state with certainty how this area of the law will evolve in the future, it does seem possible to anticipate some likely trends and suggest steps to be taken to meet them. A general statement about ascending liability can be framed in these terms: the key element in determining what, if any, legal liability a religious body may incur as a result of the action of a related college is the degree to which the religious body exerts *control* over the affairs of the college.

Imaginative plaintiffs' counsel are likely to cite precedents of agency law. Under that body of law, institutions may be liable for acts of employees performed on behalf of their employer and within the scope of their employment. In those cases, some of which involve ministers and other staff persons who have been determined to be agents of church judicatories, the courts base their decisions on the following kinds of considerations: a) who owned or controlled the property involved, b) who provided the financial resources to sustain the enterprise, c) who had the power to select or remove key employees or determine their actions while thus employed, d) to whom were the employees responsible, and e) who in fact exercised control over the activities in question.[12] These traditional agency concepts present the dilemma that insofar as the religious body attempts to exert influence upon the operations of the college in various ways, it thereby increases the risk that it will be found to have assumed liabilities which accrue to the college.

It is not possible to state with precision at what point on a spectrum of elements of influence a court will determine that a religious body has assumed liability for the acts of a college to which it is related. The matter is particularly complicated because standards governing imposition of liability vary widely from state to state, so that any generalizations must be tested against the particular law of the jurisdiction in question. Legislative action in some states has retarded the tendency to diminish or eliminate charitable immunity.[13] In other states, however, the courts have overruled legislative attempts to limit liability of charities.[14]

In general, however, for reasons stated earlier, it may be assumed that these risks are increasing for colleges and other nonprofit institutions, which in the past have been treated with a good deal of deference. In a changing judicial climate that tends to hold charitable institutions more accountable for their actions, there is real likelihood that ascending liability principles will be widely accepted.

It is true, of course, that most religious bodies and colleges will assume these risks consciously and attempt to minimize them by careful management and securing of liability insurance when it is available. It is certainly not the purpose of this study to discourage relationships between colleges and religious bodies, but rather to encourage recognition of the problems and proper initiative to meet them.

In the range of possible relationships between church and campus and of methods of achieving policy influence, some entail greater risk for a religious body than do others. For example, the four common elements of structural relationship listed in chapter one are ranked roughly in the order of their increasing likelihood of imposing liability on a sponsoring religious body. That is to say, the mere fact that a religious body has the legal right to amend or veto amendments in governing documents is quite unlikely, by itself, to impose liability. If, however, there is added to that power the ability to select enough members of the governing board to hold basic control over the affairs of the college, there is a stronger case for finding liability. If one adds to those powers the capability of entering into the management of the institution in approving or vetoing a current operating budget, an additional argument can be made that the religious body has assumed the risks which the management of any sponsoring institution incurs and should be liable to an innocent third party who is injured by actions of the college.

Plaintiffs' arguments for ascending liability based on a membership requirement either for some proportion of the members of a governing board (even for voting control) or principal officers, should not be persuasive, because there is not inherent in a membership requirement, standing alone, the kind of control implied by the power to select. Similarly, the right to prevent disposition of specified assets should not be viewed as entering into active control of the management of the college.

Even with respect to the selection of a majority of the members of a governing board, the obvious argument is available to a sponsoring religious body, that mere selection does not ensure or even imply "control," as noted above. As a matter of basic corporate law the directors are still free and indeed responsible to exercise their own independent judgment with respect to affairs of the college. Courts should accept that argument, if, in fact, the directors had been acting with such autonomy.

Again, there is a difference between potential and actual "control." The fact that a sponsoring religious body has legal powers of control may not provide a basis for the finding of ascending liability if they are never, or only rarely, exercised in the day-to-day management of the affairs of the college. It is simply not clear at this point in the development of the law what standards courts may impose.

In a recent and important case, the directors of a nonprofit hospital were found to have failed to perform their duties on a board committee by neglecting to use diligence in supervising and periodically inquiring into the actions of officers, employees, and outside experts to whom they had relegated or assigned their committee responsibilities.[15] It is thus conceivable that liability might be imposed upon a sponsoring religious body if that body failed to exercise appropriate control of a college which it dominated both legally and in operation.

An added element which has apparently never been litigated is whether the fact that various faculty or key officials of a college have accepted vows of poverty or obedience has any impact upon the issue of ascending liability. A plaintiff attempting to assert liability for the actions of those faculty or officials could be expected to argue that because of their vows such employees are even more dependent upon the employer institutions than are other employees, and because there is a substantial element of control inherent in such relations, ascending liability should be more readily imposed.[16]

Other economic and legal relationships between religious bodies and colleges will, of course, give rise to other patterns of analysis.[17] If the religious body, for example, makes substantial financial contributions on a continuing basis to the college, is a major creditor of the college or guarantor of its loans, or otherwise occupies an important economic relationship with the college, there is obviously the opportunity for influence and control as a result.[18] Further, the economic contributions of many religious bodies to their related colleges come not so much from direct as from indirect sources. For example, the religious body may be active in soliciting or encouraging contributions from other agencies and individuals on behalf of the college and may actively recruit students for the college from its members. In many instances, the very fact that there is a relationship acknowledged by the religious body makes it possible for the college to go to sources of financial support and to recruit students in ways that would be otherwise unavailable to the college.

Let us suppose that in order to effect a particular course of action on a campus, a religious body withheld direct contributions and launched a major initiative within its membership both to discourage students from attending the college and to shut off the flow of funds from any related agency or individuals with which the religious body had influence. What impact might those activities have with respect to ascending liability questions? It seems likely that the answer is not very different from that of our prior analysis. A court would consider these actions, along with all other aspects of the relationship between the institution, in making a determination of the degree and results of control which was, in fact, exercised by the religious body.

The answers are likely to turn on the relationship of such pressure by the religious body to other links of influence between the religious body and the college as well as the impact achieved on the campus. Obviously, if such actions were unsuccessful in achieving the change desired, they would be evidence of lack of control by the religious body and, therefore, evidence against the imposition of ascending liability. If, on the other hand, these actions were effective in bringing about change, they provide evidence of control. If these actions were coupled with continuing active intervention in management of the campus, the evidence of a controlled relationship would be strong. If, by contrast, this were a single incident and stood against a general pattern of autonomous action by the administrators of the campus, it would be unlikely, in and of itself, to be sufficient evidence of control by the sponsoring religious body to cause the imposition of ascending liability.

One further issue must be mentioned in this context. All individual trustees, including those representing a religious body, may incur *personal* liability for their action on behalf of the college.[19] This issue is separate from that of liability attributed to a religious body for action of college trustees, but it is a serious matter for any religious body which selects trustees to serve on college governing boards and thus benefits from their service.

Conclusion

If a religious body chooses to be involved in the life of a college or university, it must do so responsibly. Leaders of colleges and religious bodies alike should have a clear understanding of the legal consequences of their relationships and how they are structured. Problems posed by ascending liability and individual trustee liability concepts are disquieting but hardly insurmountable. In a real sense these liability considerations serve to push representatives of the college and religious body to take precautionary steps which can only be considered beneficial for the overall health of both institutions. Among those are the following:

1. The whole process of trustee selection must be taken seriously. Trustees must be chosen carefully and informed fully about their legal responsibilities and legal exposure. The most important single element in strengthening the relationships between college and religious body while at the same time reducing the risk of imposition of ascending liability on the religious body is the selection of trustees who understand and carry out their responsibilities to both institutions.

2. Trustees should be required to take part in trustee orientation programs when they are initially selected as well as periodic continuing education programs which inform and keep them up to date with respect to legal as well as other significant matters. This is vital not simply so that trustees (and administrators alike) are aware of their potential legal liabilities, but so they understand as well the limits of their legal duties and do not overreact to cries of alarm about such matters. For example, trustees should have a basic understanding of what and how matters may be delegated to college administrators, to what extent trustees may rely upon reports from those administrators in making their own decisions, what information they should demand from administrators, and what added legal responsibility trustees may assume in being assigned to certain board committees.

3. Trustees should understand the necessity of their regular attendance at trustee meetings and careful attention to the reports and other documents they receive for review. In this day no college or religious body should seek a purely ceremonial director who is chosen only for his or her name with no expectation of attendance at meetings or close attention to board work. Legal responsibilities for trustees are too substantial to permit careless handling of their duties.

4. The legal standards which apply to any particular college and its trustees are found primarily in the laws of the

state where the college is located and the governing documents of the college. All of those governing documents from the articles and bylaws of the college to the rules which determine faculty employment and student discipline matters must be reviewed periodically to ensure that they are accurate and current. In addition, all promotional documents of the college such as student catalogs and development office brochures should be reviewed with the same goal in mind.

5. Liability insurance for the college and its trustees should be reviewed periodically to ensure its adequacy, and indemnification provisions for trustees and administrators alike should be inserted into college bylaws to the extent permitted under state law.

3 Public Financial Assistance

JUST AS THE TOTAL RELATIONSHIP between college and religious body must be considered in determining questions of legal responsibility between the institutions, so also must that relationship be considered in determining whether religiously affiliated colleges are eligible for financial assistance from the government.

There is, of course, a wide variety of strongly held views among representatives of religiously affiliated higher education in this nation about financial assistance from the government—should it be accepted; if so, in what forms? Different federal constitutional limitations are likely to be imposed when government funding is provided directly to the institution rather than to the students only. Those differences will be analyzed in discussing both eligibility for public assistance in this chapter and in discussing policy influence between colleges and religious bodies in chapters five and six.

We began with the assumption that the great majority of religiously affiliated colleges in this nation accept some form of institutional aid from federal or state governments.[1] It is also true, of course, that as a matter of principle a number of institutions of higher education have refused to accept institutional aid from federal or state governments but have permitted their students to take advantage of government loan or grant programs.[2]

This study will be limited to analysis of the implications of federal support, because the standards for state support vary so dramatically. No overall pattern can be identified among the states, and there is simply no substitute for a detailed review of the constitution, legislation, case laws, and opinions of the attorney general in each state.

But a few observations might be helpful about the situation at the state level:[3]

a) The state constitutions and their interpretations are more likely to present problems for aid to independent and church related institutions of higher education than does the federal constitution. The constitutions of some states, for example, bar "lending of credit" or appropriation of money to any private institutions, whether or not church related.[4]

b) Traditions about public support for independent higher education vary widely among the states and influence both the tone of the state constitutional provisions and judicial interpretations of them. For example, the judicial decisions in Virginia tend to reflect the long history of separation of church and state there,[5] while other states with a stronger religious orientation apply more lenient standards.[6] Some western states with few private colleges tend to present the most robust prohibitions of state aid to independent institutions.[7]

c) In state court cases where the issue is interpretation of the religion clauses of a state constitution similar to those in the federal constitution, there is wide variety in the impact of the First Amendment of the federal Constitution on the parallel state constitutional provisions. Some state supreme courts will follow the United States Supreme Court's interpretation of the religion clauses of the federal Constitution, even though the provision of the state constitution may not be precisely the same.[8] Sometimes distinctions are made as to whether the aid is "direct or indirect," so that aid to students is permissible while aid to institutions is not.[9] In some states distinctions between higher education and primary and secondary education are important.[10] In some states the distinction is between institutions which are "sectarian" and those which are not.[11] In some states the prohibitions for funding church related colleges are framed in terms of forbidding any assistance "to" the colleges;[12] in other states assistance is prohibited which is "in aid of" those colleges.[13]

d) In many states, questions of aid to dependent and church related colleges and their students have not been extensively litigated;[14] some decisions on the books are of ancient vintage and little current value.[15] As aid to higher education becomes an increasingly active field for the states, one can expect greater attention to this area and more litigation which will eventually provide further guidance with respect to the permissible legal limits for public aid in the state in question. It is likely in some states which do not distinguish between primary and secondary education and higher education, that precedents will be available with respect to public support for primary and secondary schools which can be instructive for judgments about the legality of programs supporting higher education.

e) A number of states in recent years have amended their constitutions specifically to allow various forms of aid to independent or church related colleges and the students attending them, such as the student loan programs adopted in Ohio,[16] Massachusetts,[17] Texas,[18] and Georgia.[19]

In short, the state constitutions and their interpretations must be taken very seriously in examining the standards for public support, and this picture is changing constantly as a result of constitutional amendment, legislative action, and decisions of state courts.

The federal constitutional standards applied when government financial assistance is given to the institution are set forth in a trilogy of recent United States Supreme Court cases: *Tilton* v. *Richardson*, *Hunt* v. *McNair*, and *Roemer* v. *Board of Public Works of Maryland.*[20] In these cases, the Court was primarily interested in determining whether the colleges before them were carrying out their educational mission with academic integrity and thus were not so "pervasively sectarian" or permeated with religious influence that public financial assistance to them would be impermissible under the Establishment Clause of the First Amendment. In reaching this conclusion, the Supreme Court accepted the findings of the lower courts that what was taking place in those church related colleges was free academic inquiry rather than religious proselytism.

The kinds of structural relationships discussed in chapter one might be viewed as evidence of "pervasive sectarianism," in that they may reflect a marked potential for influence or control by a sponsoring religious body. It seems clear, however, that no single element of formal structural control or any combination of such elements will invalidate public funding under the standards set forth by the Supreme Court.

For example, in *Hunt* v. *McNair*, the Court upheld a South Carolina program financing construction of college facilities by tax-free revenue bonds issued by a public authority of the state. The funding challenged in *Hunt* was for the Baptist College of Charleston, a college related to the South Carolina Baptist Convention. The elements of structural control exerted by the Convention were rather stringent—all members of the board of trustees of that college were elected by the Convention, the Convention's approval was required for certain financial transactions, and the charter of the college could be amended only by the Convention.

When government funding is provided only to the students, the Supreme Court appears to have said that these structural relationships are without any significance. In *Americans United for Separation of Church and State* v. *Blanton*[21] the Supreme Court summarily affirmed the decision of a federal district court which upheld a Tennessee student assistance program giving students in that state the freedom to choose an accredited college or university, whether or not it be sectarian. The district court opinion stated:

> It should be noted here that the evidence adduced established that some, but not all, of the private schools whose students benefited from this program are operated for religious purposes, with religious requirements for students and faculty and are admittedly permeated with the dogma of the sponsoring religious organization.[22]

While the Supreme Court provided no opinion, it seems clear from the district court opinion and the documents filed by counsel with the Supreme Court, that the Court surely understood that this decision supported the right of a state to provide assistance directly to the student who attends even a pervasively sectarian institution.

Questions are frequently raised about whether certain religious activities or observances on campus will endanger eligibility for public financial assistance. In the discussion in chapter five about academic freedom, we will review the implications of religious influence in teaching and course content. Suffice it to say at this point that again the main concern of the United States Supreme Court decisions is the teaching of these courses with academic integrity rather than as an attempt to indoctrinate students to a particular faith.

Administrators at religiously affiliated colleges who wish to continue to receive public financial assistance must consider whether certain forms of religious observance jeopardize such assistance. The key to that analysis seems to be to avoid significant coercive activities which indicate an attempt to indoctrinate students to adherence to a particular belief or denominational allegiance. In the case of campus religious observances, the method of conducting the exercise is not so significant as the imposition of a compulsory requirement that a person participate in the religious observance.

The courts have consistently viewed mandatory attendance at worship services as a dispositive sign of "pervasive sectarianism" rendering both the institution and students attending them ineligible for public assistance. In *Tilton*, for example, Chief Justice Burger drew an explicit contrast between the

Connecticut colleges, none of which required attendance at religious services,[23] and the parochial schools involved in *Lemon*, which, according to the "composite profile" accepted by the Court, did require attendance at religious activities.[24] In addition to the cases directly involving public funding of education, college administrators must also consider the general reluctance of judges to sustain compulsory attendance at worhip services in any governmentally supported program.[25] In short, because the compulsion of religious belief by government is repugnant to our constitutional system, administrators at church related colleges desiring public assistance to the colleges and to their students should scrupulously avoid imposing on their faculty and student bodies regulations requiring regular attendance at worship services.

However, this conclusion does not necessarily mean that no form of mandatory prayer on a campus supported by public funds would be permissible under the Establishment Clause. Prayers at a high school commencement exercise, for example, have been sustained by a state court.[26] So have baccalaureate services preceding commencement ceremonies.[27] By the same token, a religious service at the opening of the academic year in which the faculty and student body were expected to attend would in all probability create no difficulty for the eligibility of a religiously affiliated institution to receive public assistance. The form of the prayer at such services, whether specifically denominational in character or a form of pan-ecumenical syncretism, would not be as significant as the fact that the intrusion on the belief system of the individual expected to participate is minimal.

Although the wearing of religious garb by instructors has been challenged before courts of law,[28] no court has ever ruled that this form of religious observance is sufficient warrant for declaring an institution pervasively sectarian. And in *Roemer* the Court laid this issue to rest.[29]

Finally, after *Roemer* it appears also to be permissible to begin a class with prayer if a professor so desires. Justice

Blackmun treated the issue as a facet of the instructor's academic freedom, noting that there was no "actual college policy" encouraging the practice. It is probably also prudent to add that if an individual professor desired to begin class instruction with prayer, he or she should provide an opportunity for students not wishing to participate in the exercise to absent themselves from class for the duration of the prayer. In this way the Free Exercise rights of those desiring to pray in this manner could be honored while accommodating at the same time those who would be offended by mandatory participation in the religious exercise.

Conclusion

It thus appears that under federal constitutional standards a college and religious body are free to establish virtually any formal or structural relationship they choose without endangering public assistance programs. Individual state law must always be examined, however, to determine what, if any, limitations exist thereunder.

Questions about the conduct of various forms of religious observance are not so neatly answered, but it seems apparent that while compulsory attendance at regular worship services will prove fatal to public assistance, worship at annual ceremonies such as baccalaureate services will likely pass muster. So also will the wearing of religious garb and beginning of class with prayer by an individual professor.

4 Exercise of Religious Preference in Employment Policies

A. Recent Empirical Studies

IN THE INTRODUCTION, we noted that there is considerable variety among the relationships between religious bodies and institutions of higher education. It is our assumption that where the relationship is attenuated or weak, there may not be much concern expressed either by denominational execution or by college administrators over the religious character or orientation of these employees. But where the relationship between church and campus is vivid and strong, there is deep concern over the religious character or orientation of these employees. In the words of the authors of a leading study of church-related colleges, Manning M. Pattillo, Jr., and Donald M. MacKenzie, "One of the surest means of influencing the religious character of an institution is through the appointment of staff members who share a common faith."[1]

In the fall of 1978 the Center for Constitutional Studies conducted an extensive study of administrators at religiously affiliated colleges.[2] This study disclosed an overwhelmingly positive response (91.7 percent) to the statement:

> It is important that religiously affiliated colleges and universities retain the right to exercise religious preference in faculty hiring and promotion, without thereby forfeiting their entitlement to receipt of public benefits.[3]

A lower percentage (72.6 percent) expressed agreement with a similar statement concerning religious preference in nonfaculty staff employment.

The actual practice of the institutions participating in this study did not correspond to the strong opinions about the theoretical right to exercise religious preference with respect to administrators, faculty, and nonteaching staff: Of those participating, 35.4 percent indicated that religious preference is exercised in the hiring of all administrators, and 52.2 percent indicated that such preference is exercised in filling some administrative positions, notably the offices of president (46.4 percent), vice-president (13.1 percent), and dean (18.6 percent).[4] With regard to faculty selection, 37.8 percent indicated that their general practice is to exercise religious preference in the decision to hire *all* applicants for faculty positions; 46.1 percent indicated that such preference is exercised in decisions concerning the hiring of applicants for *some* faculty positions, most notably in the departments of theology or religious studies (41.5 percent) and of philosophy (21.3 percent),[5] and 15.6 percent indicated that religious preference is never exercised in the hiring of faculty at their institutions. Although the vast majority (83.9 percent) of the institutions surveyed exercise religious preference in the selection of some or all of their faculty, only 29.1 percent stated that they exercise such preference in filling nonfaculty staff positions.[6]

The purposes of this chapter are to sketch the contours of a general argument supporting the legitimacy of religious preference at least in some instances, and to offer advice to church leaders and college administrators concerning the legal implications of an employment policy in which religious preference is a factor.

B. A Rationale for Religious Preference in Employment Policies

The phrase "religious preference" is more than a linguistic nicety. It is a necessary mode of indicating the difference between the legitimate exercise of a constitutionally protected right and invidious discrimination on the basis of race and sex. For the First Amendment protects the free exercise of religious values, while racial discrimination both by the government and in many instances by private parties not only has no support in the text of the Constitution, but is positively interdicted by the commands of the Thirteenth, Fourteenth, and Fifteenth Amendments as well as by a series of civil rights statutes enacted by Congress after the Civil War. Neither the text of the Constitution nor judicial construction of the Equal Protection Clause of the Fourteenth Amendment amount to as vigorous a prohibition against gender-based discrimination as that which obtains against racial discrimination, but the proposed Twenty-seventh Amendment (ERA), several leading Equal Protection cases, and many federal statutes in combination add up to a federal policy disfavoring irrational distinctions based on sex. In short, it is necessary to be discriminating about discrimination.

Secondly, it is important to be discriminating about the kind of religious preference practiced by institutions of higher education. As was suggested above, there is considerable variety concerning the categories of employees (administrators, faculty members, nonteaching staff persons) as to whom religious preference is exercised by these colleges and universities. It must also be stressed that religious preference need not mean that the institution prefers only members of the religious body or church to which the college is affiliated. It may mean preference for a Methodist at a Lutheran institution, or for a Baptist at a Roman Catholic institution. Or it might mean a minimal requirement that all faculty members acknowledge the legitimacy of the goals of the institution, though some of these faculty members might not incorporate those goals into the structure of their faith commitments. In short, religious preference has a polyvalent character both among institutions and within the same institution. This fact alone may have significant legal implications which will be explored later in this chapter.

A generalized rationale for some sort of religious preference may be deduced from the statement of several leaders in religiously affiliated higher education. For example, an officer of St. Olaf College, an institution closely related to the American Lutheran Church, recently stated:

> Most importantly of all, we hire people who are committed to these matters [the religious values identified with Lutheran Christianity]. All the programs and money in the world cannot help us achieve our stated ideals unless most of our faculty and administration embrace them out of conviction. When we hire, we try to hire the most capable chemists, artists or deans we can find; but we hire only those who convince us that they believe in our distinctness as a college of the Church, and who persuade us that they cherish our ideals even if they don't share our religious and ethnic heritage.[7]

Another statement of this theme was made forcefully by the Rev. James T. Burtchaell, C.S.C., who, while Provost at the University of Notre Dame, reminded his colleagues at a Mass celebrated at the opening of an academic year:

> At Notre Dame we have no task more important than to recruit and invite into our midst men and women who, beyond their being rigorously given over to the profession of learning, are likewise dedicated to a life of intelligent belief. If we are to be a Christian University, we must have a critical mass of Christian teachers. If Notre Dame is to remain Catholic, the only institutional way for assuring this is to secure a faculty with prominent representation of committed and articulate believers who purposefully seek the comradeship of others to weave their faith into the full fabric of their intellectual life.
>
> And we shall continue to need, as we have been blessed with it in the past, the companionship of believers from other religious traditions who sense and share the

> peculiar ambitions and hopes of Notre Dame. Indeed, it is of the very character of Notre Dame that teacher-scholars from so many religious traditions, and some who are not believers at all, share a common desire that this school retain its wonderful and special character. By no means need only Catholic or even Christian faculty be invited here. But by no means should anyone be invited here unaware that it is a house dedicated to intelligent belief, or indifferent to this heritage. . . .
>
> The predominating presence of Christian, Catholic scholars among our faculty, then, must be a priority of Notre Dame.[8]

These statements add up to a generalized rationale for some kinds of religious preference in the employment policies of religiously affiliated colleges. First, such preference is a manifestation of the concern of religious groups that their religious message be transmitted at the collegiate level by persons who share a commitment to this message or at least who respect the religious tradition represented by that group. Secondly, it is a way of maintaining a vivid connection between the college and its sponsoring religious body. In either instance, the rationale enjoys the constitutional support of the Free Exercise Clause of the First Amendment.[9]

We have outlined here a generalized argument in support of some kinds of religious preference at religiously affiliated colleges and universities. But this argument does not support the legal conclusion that such a college could exercise religious preference with respect to all of its employees without, for example, jeopardizing the eligibility of the institution for the receipt of public financial assistance, or without violating federal or state civil rights legislation. To assess the potential costs and benefits of an employment policy in which religious preference plays a significant role, college administrators must attend to the complicated requirements of the law as announced by Congress and the state legislatures, as interpreted by federal and state administrative and regulatory agencies, and as construed by the federal and state courts.

C. Legal Analysis

The primary focus of this section will be on the federal constitutional, statutory, and administrative requirements which are related to the issue of religious preference at religiously affiliated colleges. We include a brief sample of a few provisions of state law only to highlight the need for each college to obtain the advice of competent local counsel concerning whatever additional restraints may be imposed on these institutions by state constitutions, statutes, or administrative regulations.[10]

Our study disclosed that some religiously affiliated colleges have been willing to forego any direct financial assistance to the institution, but it disclosed none which decline to enroll students who are receiving direct federal assistance. The limitations on federal regulation of private institutions which decline public institutional assistance is a complex and important question currently under litigation,[11] but this question will not be treated here.

Because it appears to be the prevailing policy among private institutions of higher education to accept financial assistance from the federal or state government, both directly in the form of institutional support[12] and indirectly in the form of benefits to students[13] enrolled in these institutions, the model presupposed in this discussion is that of a private college which receives public support and wishes to conduct its affairs in such fashion as to be able to continue to receive this support legally.

1. Eligibility for public institutional assistance

The first question facing college administrators wishing to assert the right to exercise religious preference in their employment policies is whether in so doing they might render their institution ineligible for federal or state funding. To date, no case has squarely presented this question to the Supreme Court. But intimations of the Court's response to the question may be gleaned from three recent cases which held that both federal and state aid could flow to religiously affiliated colleges and universities without violating the Establishment Clause of the First Amendment. In this trilogy of cases the Court buttressed this conclusion with instructive dicta concerning the employment policies of the colleges involved in the lawsuits.

In *Tilton* v. *Richardson*[14] the Court sustained federal grants for the construction of academic facilities at church related colleges against a claim that such grants violated the Establishment Clause of the First Amendment. One of the arguments made against the constitutionality of the grants was that the policing of the grants by the federal government to insure that buildings constructed with federal funds were not used for sectarian purposes would engender excessive entanglement of the government with church related institutions. In his plurality opinion Chief Justice Burger rejected this contention on the theory that various factors typically present in higher education[15] diminished the risk that religion would "seep into the teaching of secular subjects."[16] In support of this conclusion the Chief Justice briefly discussed the issue of faculty hiring at the four colleges in Connecticut under scrutiny: "the faculties . . . at each [of the colleges] are predominantly Catholic. Nevertheless, the evidence shows that non-Catholics were . . . given faculty appointments. . . . Indeed, some of the required theology courses at Albertus Magnus and Sacred Heart are taught by rabbis."[17]

It would seem from *Tilton,* then, that the Court was willing to consider the religious composition of the faculty as a factor to be included in adjudicating the constitutionality of public assistance to religiously affiliated colleges. It should be added, though, that Chief Justice Burger evidently did not consider this factor to be critical, for he was willing to sustain the aid without requiring any evidence as to the extent of religious preference in the hiring or promotion process. It was enough, for example, that some "non-Catholics were . . . given faculty appointments" without any inquiry as to the number of non-Catholic faculty members, whether there was a policy against granting tenure to non-Catholics, or whether religious preference was exercised in all departments of the Catholic colleges.

In *Hunt* v. *McNair,*[18] the challenged aid was also for construction of college facilities for secular rather than sectarian use, and the Court sustained a plan to finance the construction by tax-free revenue bonds issued by a public authority of the State of South Carolina. The Court noted in passing that the college involved in the *Hunt* case was subject to substantial control by the sponsoring Baptist Church.[19] But as in *Tilton,* in *Hunt* the religious preference of faculty presented no serious question for the Court, which disposed of the issue in a single sentence: "What little there is in the record concerning the College establishes that there are no religious qualifications for faculty membership. . . ."[20]

In *Roemer* v. *Board of Public Works of Maryland*[21] the challenged aid consisted of annual noncategorical grants provided by the State of Maryland to private colleges, including religiously affiliated institutions, with a proviso that the funds could not be used by the institutions for sectarian purposes.[22] In *Roemer* the Court found that four Catholic colleges involved in the litigation were not "so permeated by religion that the secular side [could] not be separated from the sectarian."[23] In his discussion of the factors considered by the Court in reaching this conclusion, Justice Blackmun paid greater attention to religious preference in the employment of college faculty than was paid to it by the majority in *Hunt.*[24] Early in his opinion he alluded to this issue by way of an implied contrast with the state-supported elementary and secondary teachers in *Lemon* v. *Kurtzman.*[25] According to Blackmun, parochial school teachers

> were bound to mix religious teaching with secular ones, not by conscious design, perhaps, but because the mixture was inevitable when teachers (themselves usually Catholics) were "employed by a religious organization,

> subject to the direction and discipline of religious authorities, and work[ed] in a system dedicated to rearing children in a particular faith."[26]

And later in his opinion, Justice Blackmun summarized the findings of the district court on this matter:

> The District Court found that, apart from the theology departments, faculty hiring decisions are not made on a religious basis. At two of the colleges, Notre Dame and Mount Saint Mary's, no inquiry at all is made into an applicant's religion. Religious preference is to be noted on Loyola's application form, but the purpose is to allow full appreciation of the applicant's background. Loyola also attempts to employ each year two members of a particular religious order which once staffed a college recently merged with Loyola. Budgetary considerations lead the colleges generally to favor members of religious orders, who often receive less than full salary. Still, the District Court found that "academic quality" was the principal hiring criterion, and that any "hiring bias," or "effort by any defendant to stack its faculty with members of a particular religious group," would have been noticed by other faculty members, who had never been heard to complain.[27]

In summary, the *Tilton* case authorized federal aid to religiously affiliated colleges. In an opinion joined by three other justices, Chief Justice Burger spoke in terms of a predominance on the faculty of persons adhering to the community or tradition of the sponsoring religious body. The *Hunt* case approved the use of a state's ability to float revenue bonds in support of a college with clear lines of control by a religious body. But in *Hunt* Justice Powell made note of the absence of any evidence on the record concerning religious qualifications for faculty membership. In *Roemer* the Court sustained annual noncategorical grants by a state to religiously affiliated colleges. In language similar to that used by Justice Powell in *Hunt,* Justice Blackman noted that "apart from theology departments, faculty hiring decisions are not made on a religious basis." It should not be concluded from the dicta in *Hunt* and *Roemer* that the Court intended as a matter of constitutional law to place religiously affiliated colleges on the horns of a dilemma: either to abandon their right to exercise religious preference in faculty hiring or to be adjudged to be "pervasively sectarian" and thus ineligible for the governmental assistance they need to survive. These dicta appear to be casual comments on the facts before the Court in *Hunt* and *Roemer* rather than hard and fast criteria applicable to the employment policies of all religiously affiliated colleges seeking public aid. In short, it is our opinion that a college administrator may safely exercise religious preference to create a predominance of faculty members belonging to a particular religious group. In so doing, a college administrator would be relying on the language used by Chief Justice Burger in *Tilton* and would probably not jeopardize the eligibility of his institution for public assistance.

2. Eligibility for public assistance to students

Closely related to the eligibility of a religiously affiliated college for public assistance is the eligibility of its students to receive a variety of federal and state tuition grants or loans to which they have statutory entitlement. Although closely related to institutional assistance, student aid remains a distinct category for two reasons. First, it is not yet clear that aid to students at a college creates a strong enough link between the government and the college to undergird governmental regulation of the institution.[28] This means that until this question is settled, a religiously affiliated college which does not wish to subject itself to certain forms of federal regulation must avoid all receipt of direct institutional assistance, and that such an institution might be running the risk of litigation with the government if it were to administer any federally funded or assisted program of student assistance.

Secondly, in two recent decisions the Supreme Court upheld two state programs of student assistance which allowed students to participate by attending any accredited institution, public or nonpublic, within the state. In the North Carolina case, *Smith* v. *Board of Governors,*[29] the lower federal court made the following findings concerning religious preference in the selection of administrators and faculty members at a Roman Catholic affiliated college, Belmont Abbey:

> At least ten of the fourteen administrators serving from the fall of 1971 to the spring of 1976 were Catholics. Catholic preponderance on the faculty is not so great, however, though more than a majority are Catholic. At least thirty of the fifty-two members of the faculty during the 1975–76 school year were Catholic and half of those were members of the Monastery. Seventeen members of the faculty listed no religious affiliation or preference, while five indicated affiliations with other Christian denominations. In the past, the faculty has included a Jewish Rabbi and an Islamic Moslem.
>
> An applicant for a position on the faculty is not required to disclose any religious preference or affiliation, and the members of the Monastery serving on the faculty have academic qualifications comparable to the rest of the faculty members.[30]

The court made similar findings concerning religious preference at Pfeifer College, an institution affiliated with the United Methodist Church:

> Pfeifer's current President is a Methodist lay speaker. . . . Approximately one-half of the other administrators are Methodists, while 40% of those faculty members expressing a religious preference stated a preference for the Methodist Church.[31]

Finding no meaningful difference between these colleges and the Maryland institutions dealt with by the Supreme Court in *Roemer,* the *Smith* court concluded that the North

Carolina colleges "are not so pervasively religious that their secular activities cannot be separated from their sectarian ones";[32] and it upheld the flow of state funds for scholarship and tuition grants to students attending these institutions. The Supreme Court affirmed this decision summarily, or without a written opinion.

In the Tennessee case, *Americans United for the Separation of Church and State* v. *Blanton,*[33] the federal district court stated that the evidence "established that some, but not all, of the private schools whose students benefited from this program are operated for religious purposes, with *religious requirements for students and faculty* and are admittedly permeated with the dogma of the sponsoring religious organization."[34] Despite this finding of the "pervasively sectarian" character of some of the institutions where students aided by the state program were enrolled, the court thought that the child-benefit cases[35] were more closely analogous to the Tennessee program than was the *Nyquist* case, where the Supreme Court had invalidated a New York statute authorizing tuition assistance and tax relief to parents of children attending church related elementary and secondary schools.[36] Hence the court upheld the Tennessee program, noting that "total separation between church and state is not necessary. Instead, neutrality is what is required; *incidental benefits conferred on religious institutions are not proscribed.*"[37] This case clearly went beyond the Supreme Court trilogy in allowing public assistance to flow indirectly through students to "religious institutions" which were "admittedly permeated with the dogma of the sponsoring religious organization." But on the same day on which the Supreme Court upheld the *Smith* case, it likewise granted summary affirmance in the *Blanton* case.

The importance of the *Blanton* case is that the Supreme Court may be sending lower courts a message that, after reviewing several cases involving public assistance to church related higher education, it now considers the constitutional question of the permissibility of such aid closed in favor of the aid. Or it might be asserting a narrower point: that courts may be more willing to overlook the "pervasively sectarian" character of a religiously affiliated college when student aid is challenged than when direct institutional assistance is in question. In either interpretation, administrators at religiously affiliated colleges have been given an indication that they would not jeopardize the eligibility of their students to receive public assistance by maintaining a policy of religious preference in the selection of administrators and faculty members.

This conclusion appears sound to us in light of the Supreme Court's recent reaffirmation of the rule that a vote to affirm summarily is a decision on the merits of the case.[38] Summary dispositions are binding precedents which must be followed by lower courts unless and until they are reversed by the Supreme Court.

A final caution is in order, however, lest denominational executives or college administrators draw too broad a conclusion from the Supreme Court's action in *Smith* and *Blanton*. Those cases do not stand for the principle that all employees at a religiously affiliated college, including administrators, professors, and nonteaching staff, may be required to be members of a particular religion without thereby endangering the eligibility of the college for institutional assistance or the eligibility of its students for a variety of public loan and grant programs. *Smith* and *Blanton* merely represent the view of six justices that the permissibility of student aid at religiously affiliated institutions of higher education, including some "pervasively sectarian" ones with religious requirements for faculty members, did not represent a substantial federal question meriting further consideration by the Supreme Court.[39]

Neither case involved evidence of an employment policy of religious preference for nonteaching staff positions, and hence may not be relied on to support such a policy.[40] And if a case were to arise in the future involving such a practice, the Supreme Court itself would not be bound by

Smith and *Blanton* because its summary dispositions, while binding on lower courts, are not for the Supreme Court "of the same precedential value as would be an opinion of this Court treating the question of the merits."[41]

What may safely be concluded from *Smith* is what may be concluded from *Tilton:* a policy of religious preference in the selection of *administrators* and *faculty members* which results in a *preponderance* of these employees belonging to the sponsoring religious body would endanger neither institutional assistance nor aid to students attending that institution. And what may safely be concluded from the Supreme Court's summary affirmance in *Blanton* is that a policy of "*religious requirements*" for *faculty members*—the Court did not specify whether this meant some or all members of the faculty—would not endanger the eligibility of students to participate in a generalized program of assistance available to all needy students attending an accredited college, whether public, private, church related, or even pervasively sectarian in character.

What emerges from this survey of higher education funding cases is that courts look to the employment policies of religiously affiliated colleges in reaching their determinations concerning the eligibility of these institutions and their students for public financial assistance. To the best of our knowledge, no institutional aid or student assistance at the higher education level has been declared constitutionally impermissible during the past decade because of these institutions' employment policies. Hence college administrators may safely adopt policies similar to that described, for example, in *Tilton*—a predominance of faculty members of a particular religion—without fear of jeopardizing institutional assistance or student aid.

3. Compliance with federal civil rights legislation

Important as the issue of eligibility for public funding is to the survival of most religiously affiliated colleges, equal employment opportunity law must also be weighed seriously in the review of the employment policies of these institutions, irrespective of whether they accept financial aid. For this body of law affects these colleges not by way of a provision in a federal contract, but by way of a generalized law affecting nearly all employers having fifteen or more employees.[42] In constitutional language, the power asserted by Congress and upheld by the Supreme Court was not the Taxing and Spending Power (Art. I, Sec. 8, Cl. 1), but the Commerce Clause Power (Art. I, Sec. 8, Cl. 3).[43]

This section of the book attempts to clarify both what Congress intended by the Civil Rights Act of 1964 and the Equal Employment Opportunity Act of 1972 and what federal judges have said when relevant portions of those laws have come before them in litigation.

In 1964 Congress enacted a civil rights act of monumental significance. Title VII of the act covered equal employment opportunity. This title contains a general prohibition against employment discrimination based on a person's race, color, religion, sex, or national origin.[44] Had there been no other provision in the 1964 act, religiously affiliated colleges would not only have to eliminate all vestiges of racial and gender-based discrimination in their employment policies, but would also have been prohibited in exercising religious preference even in the selection of administrators and faculty members.

Section 702

The 1964 act, however, contained the following language in section 702:

> This title shall not apply to . . . a religious corporation, association or society with respect to the employment of individuals of a particular religion to perform work connected with the carrying on by such corporation, association or society of its religious activities or to an educational institution with respect to the employment of

> individuals to perform work connected with the educational activities of such institution.

The plain meaning of this provision is that Congress granted legal authority to support an employment policy whereby religious corporations, associations, or societies could legally exercise religious preference in job categories related to the religious activities of the groups. And Congress enacted a much broader provision which exempted not only religiously affiliated colleges and universities but all educational institutions from coverage under Title VII and which exempted these institutions not only from the general ban on religiously based employment discrimination but also from all forms of employment discrimination, including racial discrimination[45] and gender-based discrimination,[46] at least where the job involved work connected with an institution's educational activities.

The legislative history confirms this reading of the statute. The original version adopted by the House merely stated:

> This title shall not apply . . . to a religious corporation, association, or society.

It was on the insistence of Senators Hubert Humphrey and Everett Dirksen that this provision was limited to apply only to employees performing work connected with the religious activities of a religious corporation, association, or society.[47] The same Senators argued for adoption of the amendment extending an exemption to private educational institutions with respect to the employment of individuals to perform work connected with the educational activities of such institutions.[48]

In short, between 1964 and 1972, when the Civil Rights Act was amended, employers in a religious corporation or group could exercise religious preference if a job involved the religious activities of the group. And, subject to the provisions of Title VI, administrators at private colleges could exercise not only religious preference but also other forms of employment discrimination in hiring and promoting administrators and faculty members. On the strength of section 702, however, these administrators could not legally carry out a discriminatory policy with respect to nonteaching staff employees.

In the eight years following the passage of the 1964 act, educational institutions taken as a whole made little progress in opening up employment opportunities for women or for members of minority groups in the academy. Thus Senator Harrison Williams, the floor manager of the Equal Employment Opportunity Act of 1972, could observe:

> The existence of discrimination in the employment practices of our Nation's educational institutions is well known, and has been adequately demonstrated by overwhelming statistical evidence as well as numerous complaints from groups and individuals. Minorities and women continue to be subject to blatant discrimination in these institutions.[49]

Accordingly, the broad language of section 702 was narrowed by the 1972 amendment to read:

> This title shall not apply to a religious corporation, association, educational institution, or society with respect to the employment of individuals of a particular religion to perform work connected with the carrying on by such corporation, association, educational institution, or society of its activities.[50]

It seems clear from the legislative history of the 1972 act that the principal concern of its authors was with the overbreadth of the 1964 version of section 702. As was mentioned above, the Civil Rights Act of 1964 allowed all private colleges, whether religiously affiliated or not, an exemption from the strictures of Title VII on unfair employment practices. From the above statement of Senator Williams, one can infer that the legislative intent in 1972 was not to affect the ability of religiously affiliated colleges to exercise religious preference in faculty hiring, but to eliminate the exemption for educational institutions in the area of race and sex discrimination. Indeed, Senator Williams expressly noted in the Senate debate that there was no change introduced by the 1972 act in the language of another provision in the act, section 703 (e) (2), which in his judgment preserved fully whatever rights a church related college might wish to exercise with respect to its employment policy.[51]

The floor debate in the Senate produced one significant change in the bill. Senators Sam Ervin and James Allen challenged Senator Williams' view that these colleges were sufficiently safeguarded by leaving section 703 (e) (2) alone. Senators Ervin and Allen pointed out that the bill as reported from the Committee on Labor and Public Welfare would allow religiously affiliated colleges to exercise religious preference in hiring only on a showing that the employment position involved a *religious activity* of the college.[52] Professors of theology and religious studies would undoubtedly meet this test, as would philosophy professors, at least in a tradition where the relation between faith and reason is relatively harmonious. But on the strength of the Senate version of the bill, a college presumably could not consider the religious affiliations or convictions of a professor of a subject which is not arguably a religious activity. Thus Senator Allen objected:

> under the provisions of the bill, there would be nothing to prevent an atheist from being forced upon a religious school to teach some subject other than theology. A religious school would not like to have an atheist or people of different faith teaching other subjects and confining its right to be selective in the choice of its faculty only to those phases of the work carrying out its religious activities.[53]

To remedy this situation, Senators Ervin and Allen proposed striking the word "religious" from the term "religious activities" used in the exemption of religious educational institutions from the prohibition on sectarian hiring practices.[54]

Both authors of the amendment spoke of the detrimental impact of section 702 on religiously affiliated colleges without their proposed amendment. In a colorful colloquy the two Senators highlighted their concerns about these sorts of colleges:

> Mr. ERVIN. We have a college in North Carolina known as Davidson College that is affiliated with the Southern Presbyterian Church. Davidson College is supported by the fees of its students and by the voluntary contributions of people interested in its activities. It is not supported in any respect by the Federal Government. I happen to have had the honor to serve as a member of the board of trustees of that institution for ten years.
>
> This college was founded and is controlled by people who believe in giving a Christian education to the students of the institution—as I recall it had at the time I was a member of the board of trustees, and perhaps still has, a regulation which says that any person who is chosen to be a full professor at the institution shall be a member of an Evangelical Christian Church. Does the Senator from Alabama think that there is anything immoral or ought to be anything illegal in people who support a college devoted to giving a Christian education taking steps to assure that the youth who attend it should be instructed on any subject, whether religious or nonreligious, by teachers who are members of a Christian church?
>
> Mr. ALLEN. It seems to the junior Senator from Alabama to be a very prudent and logical requirement.
>
> Mr. ERVIN. Mr. President, I ask the Senator from Alabama whether, under the provisions of this bill, it would not be made illegal for a college which seeks to provide a Christian education at the hands of a Christian faculty in all subjects to employ in preference to an atheist, or a Mohammedan, or an agnostic, a professor to teach chemistry or educa-nomics [sic] or sociology who happened to be a member of the Christian church.
>
> Mr. ALLEN. Under this bill, I will say to the distinguished

Senator, that would be a discriminatory practice and the college could be hailed before the EEOC and ordered to cease and desist from that practice and if it did not comply with that order, it would be subject to penalty.

Mr. ERVIN. I will ask the Senator if under the provisions of the bill the Commission could not only say "Cease and desist from employing a Christian professor rather than a Mohammedan, agnostic or atheist," but the Commission could go further and say, "You have to appoint this other applicant who is a Mohammedan, agnostic, or atheist, to fill this vacant position to teach chemistry or economics or sociology and in addition you will have to pay his salary, from the time he applied for the post."

Mr. ALLEN. Under the bill, that would be possible; but with our amendment, it would not be allowed.[55]

Senator Ervin rejected Senator Williams' argument regarding the sufficiency of section 703 (e) (2) because Ervin felt that the amended section 702, to the extent that it is inconsistent with the other provision, would be regarded by the Equal Employment Opportunity Commission and by courts as the later and therefore controlling expression of congressional intent.[56] The Senate adopted the Ervin-Allen amendment without voting on it,[57] and the House accepted it as part of the recommendation of the Joint Conference Report.[58]

Another amendment proposed by Senators Ervin and Allen is equally significant in discerning the intent of Congress in the 1972 amendments. The senators proposed to exempt from the provisions of Title VII "the employment of any individuals by any educational institution or by any religious corporation, association, or society."[59] The purpose of this amendment, as expressed by Senator Ervin, was to take away the jurisdiction of the Equal Employment Commission over the employment practices of all religious corporations, associations, and societies, and all educational institutions, whether religiously affiliated or not.[60] Senator

Ervin made explicit reference to janitors[61] and secretaries[62] as job categories as to which educational institutions and religious groups might, under his amendment, legitimately exercise religious preference.

The floor manager of the bill, Senator Williams, did not accept this amendment. He urged that faculty members and nonteaching staff employees at private institutions be afforded the same protections available to public employees:

> To continue the existing exemption for these [private] employees would not only continue to work an injustice against this vital segment of our nation's work force, but would also establish a class of employers who could pursue employment policies which are otherwise prohibited by law.[63]

And he noted a broad spectrum of Christian and Jewish groups opposed the Ervin-Allen amendment.[64] The Senate rejected this amendment by a vote of fifty-five to twenty-five.[65]

In sum, from 1964 to 1972, section 702 allowed administrators at an educational institution which was incorporated as a religious corporation to exercise religious preference in an employment decision where the religious activities of the institution would be involved. And administrators at any educational institution, whether religiously affiliated or not, could have legally carried out a policy of religious preference and sex discrimination. If the institution was not the recipient of federal funds, it could also have maintained legally a policy of discrimination based on race, color, or national origin with respect to faculty members and administrative personnel. But under the 1964 act no form of employment discrimination was allowed with respect to nonteaching staff personnel.

Because of the 1972 amendments to section 702, educational institutions lost their generalized immunity from legal restraints against employment discrimination based on race, color, religion, sex, or national origin. After the adoption of the amendment, the only colleges allowed to exercise religious preference are those which can be defined as "religious educational institutions." As a result of the acceptance of the first amendment proposed by Senators Ervin and Allen, these religiously affiliated colleges may assert statutory authority for exercising religious preference with respect to all employees or prospective employees, whether or not these persons are or would become engaged in the "religious activities" of the institution. As a result of the Senate's rejection of the other Ervin-Allen amendment, however, it is clear to us that religiously affiliated colleges are limited to an exemption from the ban on religious discrimination and that they are legally bound to comply with the strictures of the act concerning employment discrimination based on race, color, sex, or national origin.

Section 703 (e) (1)

The version of the 1964 Civil Rights Act reported by the House Judiciary Committee contained not only a broad exemption from Title VII for religious corporations, associations, or societies. It also contained a provision which allows all employers, employment agencies, and labor organizations to take into account an individual's religion, sex, or national origin in cases where one or more of those categories might be a "bona fide occupational qualification reasonably necessary to the normal operation of [a] particular business or enterprise."[66]

The utility of relying on this exception, known as the BFOQ exception, depends to a large extent on the interpretation of congressional intent on the scope of the exception. On the one hand, the report of the House Judiciary Committee submitted by Congressman Peter Rodino stated that this exception was "very limited" and was available to an employer only in "those rare situations where religion or national origin is a bona fide occupational qualification."[67] This narrow construction of the availability of the BFOQ exception led Congressman Purcell to introduce an amendment to the House version which was to become section 703 (e) (2). In support of the need for his amendment, Congressman Purcell noted that religiously affiliated colleges could not rely on the BFOQ exception to exercise religious preference in all teaching positions, but only in those positions related in some way to religion:

> A church-affiliated school could probably easily defend the choice of a professor of religion, a professor of philosophy or even a professor in the social science department, on the basis of religious background and church membership. I believe, however, that a court could easily choose to interpret this law in such a way that the failure of a church-affiliated school to hire an atheist for the job of chemistry professor could subject that school to legal action.
>
> It might be equally difficult to prove that a specific religious background would be a "bona fide occupation qualification reasonably necessary," in the hiring of a dean of students, or a director of a dormitory, or even the supervisor of library materials.[68]

The chairman of the House Judiciary Committee, Emanuel Celler, was originally opposed to Purcell's amendment; and in the course of debate on the House floor he appeared to adopt a broader view of the BFOQ exception which would obviate the need for the Purcell amendment. In Celler's opinion, the BFOQ exception would be available with respect to all administrative and teaching positions.

> Now we cannot object to any bona fide occupational qualifications for positions like professors, teachers, experts, research assistants, registrars, deans or directors of dormitories.[69]

In Celler's view, the BFOQ exception would not be available with respect to nonadministrative and nonteaching staff positions: "Religion is not, and should not be a qualification for the job of janitor."[70]

Both Congressmen agreed that the BFOQ exception would not allow religious preference in nonadministrative and nonteaching positions. For Purcell this meant that another provision allowing religious preference in the choice of a laborer or a janitor by religiously affiliated colleges was necessary. Because Celler was initially opposed to the availability of religious preference with respect to these kinds of positions, he argued that the legitimate religious concerns of these institutions could adequately be met by the BFOQ exception broadly construed and that Purcell's amendment was unnecessary.

The House debate on the Purcell amendment yielded a wide variety of views argued vigorously for[71] or against[72] the wisdom of allowing religiously affiliated colleges broad discretion in the exercise of religious preference in their employment policies. Because of this divergence in views over the policy matter, a few opponents to the Purcell amendment such as Congressmen Celler, McCulloch, and Lindsay attempted to undercut support for the amendment by suggesting that the BFOQ exception was available in the filling of all administrative and teaching positions.

Whether a majority of the members of the House accepted or rejected this broad view of the exception is not clear from the record, for the Purcell amendment was eventually agreed to by Celler. There was, therefore, no vote to test whether the broad construction of this exception put forward by Celler and others in fact reflected the intent of Congress. There is clear evidence from this debate, however, that the BFOQ exception was not intended to apply to such nonadministrative and nonteaching positions as janitors, housekeepers, groundskeepers, and other laborers.

The Senate expanded the House version of the BFOQ exception by including employment agencies, labor organizations, and joint labor-management committees within the coverage of this provision. The Senate did not, however, change any other wording of this exception; nor did it during the lengthy debate on the bill shed any further light on the meaning of the BFOQ exception, which passed into law in 1964 and which was not affected by the 1972 amendments.

BFOQ and business necessity

It should be noted that equal employment law entertains a distinction between the BFOQ exception and the defense of business necessity, even though such a distinction is not immediately apparent from the language of the statute. The distinction has been illustrated in the area of sex discrimination by the authors of a leading case book on equal employment law:

> BFOQ arises only where the employer takes adverse action against or excludes males or females because of their sex: no females may work in the warehouse because the job involves lifting 100 pounds; no female with reproductive capacity may work with lead. The business necessity defense comes into play where the employer has a criterion for work in the warehouse that applicants must be able to lift 100 pounds. A rejected female applicant then claims that this is sex discrimination because it has a disparate impact on females. The employer then raises a business necessity defense, under which he must prove that the ability to lift 100 pounds is in fact reasonably necessary to performing the warehouse job.[73]

Though the distinction between BFOQ and business necessity is at times subtle, the main point of the distinction can be put simply: the BFOQ exception attends not only to what a person can do, but also to what he is. This distinction may be illustrated by the following hypothetical situations. College A, affiliated with a Southern Baptist Convention, excludes Roman Catholics from their religious studies department for a variety of reasons such as the following: (1) many of the students in this department aspire eventually to become Baptist ministers and the college wishes to have persons in that role model available to the student on a regular basis, or (2) the orthodoxy of coreligionists is more probable than with members of another religious tradition, or (3) the constituency of the sponsoring religious body which provides financial and other support to the college expects that the college will employ only Southern Baptists to teach religion. This would appear to be a perfectly acceptable BFOQ exception.

College B, a Roman Catholic university, needs to fill a position in its theology department and advertises that applicants must be familiar with the corpus of St. Thomas Aquinas. A Protestant theologian who is well qualified as a Patristics scholar but unfamiliar with Aquinas applies and is not hired. He then files an unfair employment practice charge with the EEOC, alleging that the requirement of familiarity with the writings of Aquinas has a disparate impact upon non-Catholics. Assuming that section 703 (e) (1) were the only legislation on the books, the university would still prevail by raising the defense of business necessity.

One legal scholar recently suggested that religiously affiliated colleges may rely on the BFOQ exception as the legal basis for an employment policy which does not confine the exercise of religious preference to "faculty members who teach religion, theology or philosophy" or to "chief administrative positions."[74] Although there is some evidence to support this view in some of the speeches given in the House debate, the report of the House Judiciary Committee does not support a broad construction of the BFOQ exception.[75] Both the debate and the committee report, in our opinion, preclude reliance on this exception as the legal basis for a policy of exercising religious preference with respect to positions which are not linked to the religious mission of the college. In addition, such a policy raises serious questions of constitutional law which we will attend to later in this chapter. It is sufficient to note here the existence of this additional consideration, and to conclude that if colleges should desire to exercise religious preference in all employment positions, the statutory authority for such a policy is not the BFOQ exception, section 703 (e) (1), but the exemption provided in section 702, or the exception provided for some religiously affiliated colleges in section 703 (e) (2).

Section 703 (e) (2)

As was mentioned above, the version of the Civil Rights Act of 1964 reported by the House Judiciary Committee did not contain any explicit references to religiously affiliated colleges and universities. By accepting the Purcell amendment the House agreed to add the following language to the exception clause:

> it shall not be unlawful employment practice for a school, college, university, or other educational institution or institution of learning to hire and employ employees of a particular religion if such school, college, university, or other educational institution or institution of learning is, in whole or in substantial part, owned, supported, controlled, or managed by a particular religion or by a particular religious corporation, association or society, or if the curriculum of such school, college, university, or other educational institution or institution of learning is directed toward the propagation of a particular religion.[76]

The scope of the exception provided by the addition of these words is plainly limited to religious preference. Several supporters of the Purcell amendment emphasized during the House debate that there was intent to countenance racial discrimination by these colleges. Congressman Quie, for example, stated: "There is nothing in this amendment which goes to the question of race, color, or national origin."[77] And he noted that if a religiously affiliated college accepts federal funds, it would be bound by the provisions of Title VI banning discrimination on the basis of race, color, or national origin.

As was suggested in the discussion of the BFOQ exception, the kinds of employees intended to be covered by this provision is all-inclusive. In support of his amendment, Congressman Purcell stated:

> There may be some who feel that it would be an unwise policy for a church-affiliated school to restrict itself only to members of its own church for its employees, but certainly it should be their right to do so. . . . The

> church-related school should never be called upon to hire an atheist or a member of a different faith. . . . It should be spelled out that there is no question of their right to hire employees on the basis of religion.[78]

Other supporters of the amendment likewise reflected the view of the author of the amendment that religiously affiliated colleges should be granted statutory authorization to take into consideration the religious background or orientation of all their employees or prospective employees without violating the civil rights law.[79] Section 703 (e) (2) was enacted into law in 1964 and was unaffected by the 1972 amendments.

Once again it is important to note that this broad exception, applicable to all employment positions, whether or not there is any nexus between the job and the religious activities of the college, may be subject to constitutional challenge. Further constitutional issues are presented by the wording of section 703 (e) (2), which is available only to colleges which meet one of the following two criteria: (1) ownership, support, control, or management in whole or in substantial part by a religious corporation, association, or society, or (2) orientation of curriculum toward the propagation of a particular religion.

The very fulfillment of the first criterion—ownership, support, control, or management—may present a problem for the eligibility of a college to receive public institutional assistance, for it may seem to some judges to be a statement of an institution's pervasively sectarian character. And the second criterion—orientation of curriculum—likewise raises a similar problem.

The legislative history of Title VII, both in the 1964 version and its subsequent amendment in 1972, does not contain even the intimation of an opinion concerning the constitutionality of public assistance to church related colleges. The main thrust of Title VII was to provide effective civil rights legislation concerning equal employment opportunity, not to decide which kinds of institutions might permissibly receive federal assistance. Even if the authors of Title VII had considered the church-state questions lurking beneath the surface of sections 702 and 703 (e) (2), they would have done so without the benefit of any of the most relevant decisions of the Supreme Court, which began in 1971, seven years after the enactment of the Civil Rights Act of 1964.

4. Judicial interpretation of the civil rights law

If administrators of church related colleges want to adopt or reformulate employment policies in which religious preference plays a significant role, they must attend not only to what Congress may have thought the Constitution required of them in 1964 and 1972, but also to what the federal courts have said about constitutional constraints governing the eligibility of these institutions for public assistance and the legitimacy of the congressional enactments allowing religious preference in employment decisions at these colleges.

Implications for eligibility for public funding

We have already considered the implications of the public funding cases for the employment policies of religiously affiliated colleges wishing to exercise religious preference. It should suffice here to consider whether language in the statutory provisions allowing religious preference by these colleges would create any further constitutional difficulty.

Section 702 speaks of a "religious educational institution." A college which wishes to rely on this statutory provision to support its employment policy would probably not jeopardize its eligibility for public assistance merely by asserting section 702 as a defense in an employment discrimination case.

Section 702 (e) (2), however, contains language which may create a dilemma for this sort of college. We have seen in the Introduction and in chapter one that a variety of legal and structural relationships exist between church and campus in this country. And in chapter three it was noted that Justice Powell intimated in *Hunt* v. *McNair* that control of a college by a church body would not, by itself, render that institution ineligible for public financial assistance. It is conceivable, however, that if a college relies on section 703(e)(2) in an employment dispute, it may find itself the target of litigation by a taxpayer or of an administrative proceeding by a governmental agency seeking to cut off funds to the institution on the theory that the "wall of separation" prohibits the flow of public money to an institution which is "owned, supported, controlled, or managed by a particular religious corporation, association, or society."

The second test found in section 703(e)(2) is similarly troublesome. For to gain the exception made available by the statute, a college must concede too much if it wishes to remain eligible for public assistance. By stating that its curriculum "is directed toward the propagation of a particular religion," the college may appear to have acknowledged its "pervasively sectarian character" and thus to have rendered itself vulnerable to the claim that it is ineligible to receive federal and state subsidies to which it would otherwise be entitled.

The apparent dilemma created by the language of Title VII suggests the need for a legislative amendment which would protect the right of religiously affiliated colleges to preserve their religious integrity without foregoing benefits they may need to survive. We do not wish to exaggerate the possibility that reliance by a college on the statutory defenses in Title VII would by that fact alone jeopardize its eligibility for public assistance. If such a barrier was erected because of the poor choice of words in Title VII, it would not be insurmountable. If confronted by claims that the management of a college by a church or the orientation of its curriculum towards religious values renders that college ineligible for public aid, the college may rebut these claims by demonstrating that its relationship with the church or religious body does not destroy the academic integrity of the college's educational function and that its transmission of religious values is legitimate witness rather than coercive proselytizing.

Constitutionality of Title VII exemption and exception

From 1964 to 1972 the law governing religious preference by religious employers was in a state of confusion created by the Congress itself. On the one hand, section 702 limited religious preference to employees engaged in the "religious activities" of the religious institution. On the other hand, section 703 (e) (2) allowed religiously affiliated colleges to exercise religious preference in filling all positions, whether or not related to the religious goals or mission of the college. After 1972 this legislative confusion was resolved by the adoption of the first Ervin-Allen amendment, for by deleting "religious" as a modifier of the activities which an employee of a particular religion could be hired to perform, Senator Ervin's amendment brought section 702 into conformity with the intent of Congress in passing section 703 (e) (2) in 1964.

Shortly after the passage of the 1972 amendment, but before there was any opportunity to take this enactment into account, the Fifth Circuit Court of Appeals handed down its decision in *McClure* v. *Salvation Army,*[80] the first appellate court decision involving a claim of sex discrimination and a defense resting on the exemption provided to religious bodies in section 702. Miss Billie B. McClure, a female minister, was ruled to be an "employee" within the meaning of Title VII for the purpose of complaining that her "employer," the church in which she was ordained, had unlawfully practiced gender-based discrimination by offering male ministers higher salary and other benefits. Rather than deciding the constitutional question of whether the statute had a valid secular purpose and primary effect, the Fifth Circuit sustained the dismissal of the plaintiff's complaint on the strength of the principle that a secular court should not attempt to resolve civil disputes which engage the court "in the forbidden process of interpreting and weighing church doctrine."[81] As Judge Coleman stated:

> An application of the provisions of Title VII to the employment relationship between . . . a church and its minister would . . . cause the State to intrude upon matters of church administration and government which have so many times before been proclaimed to be matters of a singular ecclesiastical concern. . . . The Church would then be without the power to decide for itself, free from state interference, matters of church administration and government.
>
> Moreover, in addition to injecting the State into substantive ecclesiastical matters, an investigation and review of such matters of church administration and government as a minister's salary, his place of assignment and his duty, which involve a person at the heart of any religious organization, could only produce by its coercive effect the very opposite of that separation of church and State contemplated by the First Amendment.[82]

Limiting its decision to the specific factual pattern before it, the Court ruled that "Congress did not intend, through the nonspecific wording of the applicable provisions of Title VII, to regulate the employment relationship between church and minister."[83]

In the only other appellate decision involving section 702, a direct challenge was made to the legitimacy of the broad exemption enacted by Congress in the 1972 version of this provision. In *King's Garden, Inc.* v. *FCC*[84] an applicant for employment at a radio station owned and operated by a religious organization complained to the Federal Communications Commission that the station had unlawfully discriminated against him on the basis of religion. The job applicant had been asked questions such as "Are you a Christian?" and "Is your spouse a Christian?" The Commission ruled that the religious organization could ask such questions only of "persons hired to espouse a particular religious philosophy over the air."[85] On appeal, the religious organization argued that the 1972 amendment to Title VII required that the FCC amend its rules which bar broadcast licensees from discriminating in employment on the basis of religion[86] to allow religious preference in hiring by a religious corporation, association, educational institution, or society.

Judge Skelly Wright, currently the Chief Judge of the D.C. Circuit, wrote the opinion of the court which rejected the radio station's contentions. In reaching the conclusion that the religious corporation was not exempt under the act from the general ban against employment discrimination on the basis of religion, Judge Wright relied in part on the legislative history of the statute, noting that Congress had given "absolutely no indication that it wished to impose the [702] exemption upon the FCC"[87] and that the sponsors of the 1972 exemption were chiefly concerned to preserve the statutory power of sectarian schools and colleges to discriminate on religious grounds in the hiring of all of their employees."[88]

Although Judge Wright grounded his decision on the power of the FCC to regulate with respect to broadcasting, he added a detailed constitutional analysis of the statute which has ramifications for religiously affiliated higher education as well as for broadcasting. In this section of his opinion Judge Wright wrote: "The 1972 exemption is of very doubtful constitutionality."[89] The judge opined that the statute could not be sustained under the Establishment Clause of the First Amendment and that it would not withstand equal protection analysis under the Fifth Amendment. Employing the familiar tests enunciated by the Supreme Court in First Amendment cases, he wrote that neither he nor his colleagues, Judge Bazelon and Judge Wyzanski, could conceive of a valid secular purpose served by the "unbounded exemption" of the 1972 amendment which did not require a showing that the job involved a religious activity of the religious corporation. Secondly, he intimated that the statute would fall under the primary effect test as well, for the 1972 exemption "invites religious groups, and them alone, to impress a test of faith on job categories, and indeed whole enterprises, having nothing to do with the exercise of religion."[90] In creating a "gross distinction between the rules facing religious and non-religious enterpreneurs," he concluded, "Congress placed itself on collision course with the Establishment Clause."[91]

Finally, Judge Wright asserted that the statute worked an invidious discrimination prohibited by the Due Process Clause of the Fifth Amendment. For, in his opinion, "the criterion of discrimination–i.e., the religious or nonreligious character of the owning or operating group–not only lacks a rational connection with any permissible legislative purpose, but is also inherently suspect."[92] Judge Wright then ruled that, under the applicable rules of the FCC, the radio station was prohibited from engaging in sectarian hiring of persons not involved in the process of articulating a particular religious philosophy over the air.[93]

Judge Bazelon, who was the Chief Judge of the D. C. Circuit at the time the opinion was written, concurred in the judgment of the court but added an opinion stating that he disagreed with Judges Wright and Wyzanski as to the method they had used to avoid constitutional adjudication. Persuaded that the FCC cannot "impose employment requirements in direct conflict with the standards established by Congress,"[94] and stating that he was convinced by Judge Wright's constitutional analysis of the statute, Judge Bazelon stated that he would hold the exemption unconstitutional. The decision of the D.C. Circuit was appealed to the Supreme Court, but the Court let the decision stand by denying the writ of certiorari.[95]

Neither *McClure* nor *King's Garden* involved a religiously affiliated college. But if applied to the context of the employment policy of such a college, *McClure* would support the BFOQ exception, which is available when there is a demonstrable nexus between a particular job and the religious mission of the college. For example, under *McClure*, it seems clear that a religiously affiliated college may take into account the church membership or religious orientation of a campus minister or a theology professor. It seems likewise clear from both *McClure* and *King's Garden* and from *Wisconsin* v. *Yoder*[96] that a college closely related to a church or religious group, like the Hasidic Jews or the Old Order Amish, which teaches a religious duty of isolation of its members from secular society would be in a strong position to assert a Free Exercise claim in support of a policy of religious preference with respect to all its employees. Under *King's Garden*, however, a college related to a church which does not espouse a tenet of isolation of its members from secular society could not rely on section 702 or 703 (e) (2) to support the exercise of religious preference in relatively low level staff positions which do not implicate the employee in the religious mission of the college in a demonstrable fashion. Under those circumstances, it would seem that the generalized right of the employee to be free from religious discrimination in the job market would probably prevail over a Free Exercise claim asserted by a religiously affiliated college.

5. Administrative regulations

Another source of law governing religious preference in employment policies of religiously affiliated colleges is the body of rules which emanates from federal administrative and regulatory agencies set up to implement the general designs of Congress. We offer here three examples of such agencies: the Equal Employment Opportunity Commission, the Office for Federal Contract Compliance Programs, and the Internal Revenue Service.

EEOC regulations and decisions

The authors of this study are aware of no EEOC decision applying section 702 or 703 (e) (2) to a religiously affiliated college in the context of a policy or practice to exercise religious preference in the hiring and promotion of faculty and other personnel. But the Commission has relied on these provisions in a case involving a charge of an unfair employment practice against a Christian school at the pre-elementary level for its refusal to hire the charging party because of her Jewish religion. Noting that the school provides to preschool through second grade children "educational opportunities undergirded by sound Christian principles and teachings as found in the Bible," the Commission found that the school met both prongs of the 703 (e) (2) test: it was "wholly owned, supported, controlled, and managed by the Church": and religion occupies "an integral part of the child's daily life at school." Citing both section 702 and section 703 (e) (2), the Commission ruled that there is no reasonable cause to believe that Charging Party and other Jewish applicants are "unlawfully excluded by the school from consideration of hiring and actual hiring because of their religion."[97]

Like the parallel provisions in sections 702 and 703 (e) (2), the religion BFOQ exception has not been the subject of many reported decisions by the EEOC. As of 1979 the only case involving alleged discrimination on the basis of religion which was resolved by use of the BFOQ exception was an unreported decision in 1977. The case involved the hiring of a biology professor, partly because of that person's religious affiliation. And an EEOC district director ruled that a religiously affiliated college could rely on the BFOQ exception as a legitimate reason for the selection.

In the general treatment of the BFOQ exception in an earlier part of this chapter, it was noted that there is some basis in the legislative history to support the view that religiously affiliated colleges may use the BFOQ exception to exercise religious preference in filling all teaching positions. This interpretation, however, does not enjoy the support of the accompanying committee report which described the exception as "very limited" to "rare circumstances." Furthermore, although the EEOC has not yet issued guidelines construing the religion BFOQ, it has announced that it intends to construe the other two provisions of section 703 (e) (1) strictly. The Commission first announced its rule of strict construction of the BFOQ exception in guidelines issued in 1970 concerning discrimination because of national origin.[98] Two years later the Commission issued guidelines on discrimination because of sex which stated that the BFOQ exception as to sex "should be interpreted narrowly."[99] This narrow construction of the BFOQ exception has been adopted by the Supreme Court in its adjudication of employment discrimination cases.[100] These factors yield the conclusion suggested earlier: that administrators of religiously affiliated colleges cannot rely on the religion BFOQ unless there is some demonstrable link between the employment position as to which religious preference is exercised and the religious activities or goals of the college.

Reasonable accommodation of religious practices

As was suggested above, the EEOC has never issued guidelines construing the meaning of the religion BFOQ exception. But in 1967 it issued guidelines on discrimination because of religion which imposed on all employers covered by Title VII a duty "to make reasonable accommodations to the religious needs of employees and prospective employees where such accommodations can be made without undue hardships on the conduct of the employer's business."[101] The guidelines were issued in response to several complaints which raised the question whether an employer would be involved in unlawful religious discrimination if he discharged or failed to hire employees who regularly observe their Sabbath on some day other than Sunday and who observe other religious holidays throughout the year.

After litigation challenging the authority of the EEOC to promulgate this regulation, Congress supported the view adopted by the Commission by amending Title VII in 1972 to include a definition of religion which included "all aspects of religious observance and practice, as well as belief, unless an employer demonstrates that he is unable to reasonably accommodate to an employee's or prospective employee's religious observance or practice without undue hardship on the conduct of the employer's business."[102]

Subsequent to the passage of this amendment, there has been further litigation testing the meaning of "undue hardship." The regulation suggested that undue hardship "may exist where the employee's needed work cannot be performed by another employee of substantially similar qualifications during the period of absence of the Sabbath observer." In a recent decision involving the religious beliefs of an employee who sought Saturdays off in accordance with the religious tenets of his church, the Supreme Court ruled by a vote of seven to two that an employer had made adequate efforts to accommodate those beliefs merely by authorizing a union steward to search for someone who might exchange shifts. According to the Court, the employer's duty to accommodate religious beliefs and practices does not require him to take steps inconsistent with an otherwise valid collective bargaining agreement, or to bear more than a "de minimis" cost in order to give an employee Saturdays off.[103]

Some commentators have criticized the Court for appearing to minimize the value of religious freedom of employees who do not conform to the mainstream religious practices of this country. In any event, the 1972 amendments to Title VII make it plain that all employers covered by the act must make reasonable efforts to accommodate the religious practices of their employees. Although the Supreme Court did not construe this provision of Title VII very broadly, it did not, on the other hand, invalidate it. It remains the law of the land, and there is no exemption from it available to religiously affiliated colleges. Indeed, it would be inconsistent to argue for such an exemption on First Amendment grounds, for the Free Exercise Clause is the basis both of the college's desire to exercise religious preference in some of their employment practices and of some employees' desire for reasonable accommodation in their work schedules.

What this statutory provision requires, then, is that administrators at religiously affiliated colleges make bona fide efforts to arrange alternative work schedules, for example, for Jewish employees wishing to observe holidays like Yom Kippur, Muslims who do not wish to work on Fridays, or Seventh-Day Adventists and Jews who do not wish to work on Saturdays. Academic schedules are often flexible enough to meet a variety of nonreligious needs or desires of professors. Hence we see no reason why an attitude of flexibility ought not also prevail when the need for accommodation is religiously grounded.

Executive Order 11246 and OFCCP regulations

Another area of administrative regulation impacting upon all religiously affiliated colleges which maintain contracts or subcontracts with the federal government is the enforcement of Executive Order 11246, as amended.[104] This Executive Order requires virtually all contracts or subcontracts with the federal government to include a nondiscrimination clause, according to which the contractors agree as follows:

> The contractor will not discriminate against any employee or applicant for employment because of . . . religion. . . . The contractor will take affirmative action to ensure that applicants are employed, and that employees are treated during employment, without regard to their . . . religion. . . .[105]

The penalty for noncompliance with the nondiscrimination clause is cancellation, termination, or suspension of the contract(s) in whole or in part and declaration that the contractor is ineligible for further contracts with the federal government.[106]

While the Executive Order was enforced according to these terms, officials at church related colleges and universities complained to the Office of Federal Contract Compliance Programs (OFCCP) in the Department of Labor and to the Congress that these provisions laid more onerous obligations on the colleges than did the terms of the civil rights legislation, and that, as applied to the exercise of religious preference in the recruitment and selection of faculty, they abridged the constitutional rights of these colleges to free exercise of religion and freedom of association.[107]

In response to these complaints, in 1975 OFCCP amended its regulations construing the relevant Executive Orders. The governing regulations now follow almost verbatim the language of the exemption in section 703 (e) (2) of the Civil Rights Act:

> It shall not be a violation of the equal opportunity clause for a school, college, university, or other educational institution or institution of learning to hire and employ employees of a particular religion if such school, college, university, or other educational institution or institution of learning is, in whole or in substantial part, owned, supported, controlled, or managed by a particular religion or by a particular religious corporation, association, or society, or if the curriculum of such school, college, university, or other educational institution or institution of learning is directed toward the propagation of the particular religion. The primary thrust of this provision is directed at religiously oriented church-related colleges and universities and should be so interpreted.[108]

Another regulation prohibiting employment discrimination on the basis of religion or national origin was amended at the same time to eliminate any possibility of an administrative interpretation conflicting with the language of the above regulation.[109]

The difficulty with the Department of Labor's administrative rule on this subject is four-fold. First, the text of the Executive Order itself was not amended to conform to the interpretation announced by the Department in 1975. Secondly, one consequence of tracking the language of section 703 (e) (2) of the Civil Rights Act is that the Department's interpretation does not extend an exception to those religiously affiliated or committed colleges which cannot accurately be described either as "owned, supported, controlled, or managed by a particular religious corporation, association, or society" or as directed in their curriculum "toward the propagation of [a] particular religion." Thirdly, the regulation does not take into account the constitutional limits cautioned by Judge Wright in the *King's Garden.* And fourthly, the regulation does not illustrate by example what is meant by a federal "contract" or "subcontract." A clear example of a contract would be a research grant provided by the federal government to a department or a subunit of a college. Much less clear is whether the government would likewise maintain that all financial assistance made available to students puts the indirect beneficiary, the college, into a contractual relationship with the government. The view sketched above in part one and two of this chapter suggests that the Supreme Court looks differently upon institutional assistance and student aid, and the *Grove City College* case presents a direct challenge to the government's assertion of jurisdiction over the institution via student aid. The outcome of this litigation may have important consequences for the interpretation of federal contracts.

IRS rulings and regulations

A third instance of a federal agency which has at least the potential to affect the employment policy of church related colleges is the Internal Revenue Service. For by issuing a revenue ruling or a revenue procedure concerning the tax-exempt status of these institutions under section 501 (c) (3) of the Internal Revenue Code, the Service could dry up a major source of the financial support upon which these institutions rely for their survival: tax-deductible contributions.

To date, however, the IRS has not adversely affected these colleges by issuing any regulation affecting their ability to exercise religious preference in their employment practices. And it seems highly unlikely to do so in the future. This prediction seems probable because of the rationale relied upon by the IRS when it announced its decision in 1971 denying tax-exempt status to schools which maintain a racially discriminatory policy as to their students. The ruling referred to the general common law governing charitable trusts and stated that an organization would not qualify as charitable if its activities were either illegal or contrary to public policy.[110]

It seems clear from the review of federal civil rights legislation in part three of this chapter that there is no public policy against the exercise of religious preference in employment by religiously affiliated colleges, at least with respect to positions implicating the religious mission of the college. On the other hand a review of the same statutes discloses a clear policy against racial discrimination in education.[111] Hence it would not be irrational or inconsistent for the IRS to uphold tax-exempt status in the former instance while denying it in the latter.

In 1975 the IRS issued guidelines for determining whether private schools qualify for tax-exempt status on the basis of the school's policy on racial nondiscrimination in student admissions. Included in these guidelines was a statement on employment of faculty and administrative staff as an indicator of the school's policy with respect to students:

> The existence of a racially discriminatory policy with respect to employment of faculty and administrative staff is indicative of a racially discriminatory policy as to students. Conversely, the absence of racial discrimination in employment of faculty and administrative staff is indicative of a racially nondiscriminatory policy as to students.[112]

It should be repeated that neither the 1971 revenue ruling nor the 1975 revenue procedure dealt directly with religious preference in faculty hiring. Because the IRS has dealt with the tax-exempt status of private schools chiefly in the context of student admissions, the potential impact of the IRS on church related colleges will be treated in greater detail in the next chapter of this volume.

6. Compliance with state constitutions and civil rights enactments

The focus of the legal analysis throughout this chapter has been on the implications of the federal civil rights legislation and other federal statutes and regulations for the policies of religiously affiliated colleges. The constitutions, statutes, and regulations of the several states pose additional legal problems of such variety and magnitude as to require treatment in a separate volume. It should suffice here to call attention once again to Professor Howard's excellent state-by-state review of legal problems relating to public funding of independent colleges,[113] and to urge college administrators to consult with competent local counsel concerning the requirements not only for eligibility of the institution for public financial assistance but also for compliance with state civil rights legislation and other laws affecting the college.

To underline the need for consultation with experienced local counsel, we wish to stress here that different standards obtain between federal and state requirements as well as among the enactments of the several states. It was suggested above that relying on section 703 (e) (2) of the federal Civil Rights Act of 1964 would probably not endanger the eligibility of an institution for the receipt of federal funding. This conclusion was based on the fact that ownership, management, and control of an educational institution by a religious body would not be taken by federal courts to be as significant as the degree of open academic inquiry on the campus. The same conclusion does not follow for religiously affiliated colleges in New York, for the constitution of that state explicitly prohibits the use of "any public money . . . directly or indirectly, in aid or maintenance, other than for examination or inspection, of any school . . . wholly or in part under the control or direction of any religious denomination, or in which any denominational tenet or doctrine is taught. . . ."[114] In order to qualify for state institutional assistance in New York, a religiously affiliated college must pay careful attention not only to what is taught and how it is taught on campus, but also to how the relationship between church and campus is legally described.[115]

Another example should suffice to illustrate the often striking difference between federal and state legislation. As we have seen above, the 1964 Civil Rights Act, as amended, allows religiously affiliated colleges to exercise religious preference in their employment practices. The equal protection clause of the New York Constitution, however, appears on its face to exclude such religious preference: "No person shall, because of race, color, creed or *religion*, be subjected to any discrimination in his civil rights by any other person, or by any firm, corporation, or institution. . . ."[116]

Finally, it should be noted that there is considerable variety among the civil rights laws of the several states. Although the National Commission on Uniform State Law has proposed a Model Anti-Discrimination Act[117] for the consideration of the state legislatures, only a few states have adopted this act in its entirety. One state, Maryland, has adopted an exemption provision akin to section 702 of the federal civil rights law.[118] Other states have adopted the BFOQ portion of the Model Act, akin to section 703 (e) (1) of the federal civil rights law.[119] Still others have adopted the provision akin to section 703 (e) (2) of the federal civil rights law.[120] In short, there is no substitute for informed advice from local counsel concerning the implications of state law for the employment policy of a religiously affiliated college.

D. Summary and Conclusion

In this chapter we have seen that there are a variety of complex legal judgments which must be made in the formulation and implementation of employment policy at a religiously affiliated college. From recent Supreme Court cases we have learned that under federal standards this kind of college would not by the exercise of religious preference in selection of its faculty and administrative staff forfeit eligibility to receive public institutional assistance, and that such a policy would not endanger the eligibility of its students for public financial assistance. In the review of the statutory provisions we saw that since 1972 Congress authorized religious educational institutions to exercise religious preference in the selection of all their employees, and that since 1964 Congress has authorized a BFOQ exception, whereby all employers are granted a limited exception to take the religion of their employees into account in relatively confined instances. Religiously affiliated colleges or universities, defined by a relationship of ownership, management, or control by a church and by a curriculum content directed to propagation of the religious tenets of the sponsoring church, were granted a broader ability to exercise religious preference in the selection of all their employees.

The very statement of these statutory provisions or the application of their language to religiously affiliated colleges creates two constitutional difficulties. First, reliance on the statutory defenses provided in Title VII could make a religiously affiliated college vulnerable to a challenge of its eligibility for public financial assistance, on the ground that the language of Title VII describes institutions which are pervasively sectarian. The central defense to such a challenge rests on the ability to demonstrate that instruction on the campus occurs within a context of genuine academic freedom rather than one of coercive proselytizing.

Secondly, there has been important litigation about the constitutionality of parts of Title VII. We saw that one view of the First Amendment—that it enacts a wall of separation between Church and State—led various Congressmen to enact a sweeping exemption of religious educational institutions from the general prohibition against employment discrimination on the basis of religion. And we saw another view of the First Amendment articulated in the *King's Garden* case. In the view of three eminent judges, a generalized policy of religious discrimination in employment up and down the line would violate the Constitution. Although this opinion does not represent the law of the land, it does represent a storm warning which may not be ignored.

Our own conclusion from this complex body of law is that if administrators of religiously affiliated colleges wish to assert a right of religious preference where there is no demonstrable nexus between the employment position in question and the religious mission of the college, they must be prepared to risk litigation which would test the constitutional validity of the broad statutory exemption of these institutions from the law prohibiting religious discrimination. In our opinion such litigation would probably result in a narrowing of the statutory exemption or its invalidation. We also believe that it is not constitutionally permissible to grant religiously affiliated colleges an absolute immunity from the general prohibition against employment discrimination on the basis of religion, because the duty of the courts is to protect both the religious interests of these institutional employers and the religious freedom of their employees or prospective employees.

5 Academic Freedom

IN THE PREVIOUS CHAPTER we suggested that the primary reason offered for the legitimacy of religious preference in faculty selection is the need for religiously affiliated colleges to staff their institutions with persons committed to or at least sympathetic with the religious goals involved in this kind of educational experience. In other words, religious bodies engaged in higher education are exempt from an otherwise applicable ban on religious discrimination in employment practices, because such an exemption is necessary if these institutions are to preserve their religious character and identity. The focus of the last chapter was on the selection of men and women for faculty and administrative positions. In this chapter we focus on the process of promotion of faculty members, termination of their services, or the invocation of other sanctions for failure to conform to religiously based goals maintained by church related colleges, and on the limits imposed on this process by commonly accepted norms concerning academic freedom.

We note at the outset that we are not aware of any evidence that religiously affiliated colleges experience difficulties in the area of academic freedom with any greater relative frequency or seriousness than do their public and independent counterparts.[1] We likewise note that many of the problems of academic due process which have occurred at religiously affiliated colleges under the rubric of academic freedom have arisen not because of a conflict between the prerogatives of professors in their classrooms and the institution's commitment to religious values, but because of a dispute over appropriate arrangements to be made concerning the termination of professors in a time of financial exigency.[2] Some problems of academic freedom, however, are unique to religiously affiliated colleges because they emerge as problems only because of the specifically religious character of the institution and its desire to assert a religious influence over curriculum and course content.[3] The focus of this chapter is solely on these sorts of problems and on the implications which these problems suggest for the eligibility of religiously affiliated colleges and their students to receive public financial assistance.

A. The Practice of Academic Freedom at Religiously Affiliated Colleges

The survey of administrators of religiously affiliated colleges which we conducted in the fall of 1978 disclosed that 83.9 percent of the respondents exercise religious preference in the selection of some or all of their faculty. Such preference, however, does not play as significant a role in decision to grant tenure to a faculty person. Of the respondents 68.1 percent indicated that religious preference is not exercised at all in the tenure decision; 25.3 percent stated that they do exercise religious preference in all tenure decisions; and 6.6 percent exercise religious preference in some tenure decisions, notably in the departments of theology or religious studies and of philosophy.[4]

One indicator of the seriousness with which the administration of a religiously affiliated college views the belief structure or ethical values of its faculty is the inclusion of a provision in standard employment contracts requiring adherence to or respect for the beliefs or values taught by the religious body with which the college is affiliated. Our survey disclosed that some such provision appears in all contracts of employment, including those of faculty members, at 32.2 percent of the responding institutions. Only seven institutions (4.8 percent) indicated that there was any occasion during the past five academic years (1973–1978) to enforce this provision.

One of the respondents to our survey, an administrator at William Jewell College in Liberty, Missouri, indicated that his college utilizes a merit system in granting promotion and tenure. According to this system a professor being evaluated for promotion or tenure must demonstrate that he possesses not only teaching competence, professional education, advisory effectiveness, scholarly achievement, and contribution to the college, but also "commitment to the Christian character of William Jewell College" as described in the college's official Statement of Purpose. That statement indicates that the college is committed:

> To be an institution with unquestioned loyalty to the ideals of Christ, which includes a Christian philosophy in teaching and in daily living on the campus. The college aspires to be a community in which the Christian commitment of the members exemplifies the compatibility of sound scholarship and the Christian faith, and demonstrates its worthiness as a way of life. In keeping with this viewpoint the individual is challenged to develop a worthy code of conduct for his life which should inspire him to meaningful involvement with his fellow man.
>
> To cooperate thoroughly with the Missouri Baptist Convention to offer the finest Christian education possible. As a church related institution, William Jewell College, founded in 1849 by the Baptists of Missouri, who have continued to provide financial support, aims to serve the denomination and to emphasize the best in its Baptist heritage. The college helps train leaders both professional and non-professional, for the denomination and seeks new methods of communicating the Christian faith to each generation.[5]

Whether to meet the expectations of a religious body which supports a college financially or simply "to be an institution with unquestioned loyalty to the ideals of Christ," some religiously affiliated colleges maintain a practice of exercising religious preference not only in the selection of their faculty members, but also in decisions concerning which faculty members are to be granted promotion and tenure, and, by implication, which faculty members are to be terminated.

Does such a policy create any legal difficulties for a college which wishes to remain eligible for public financial assistance? Does such a policy create further difficulties for a college if a professor terminated for some religiously based reason decides to litigate concerning his employment contract? Are there any limitations on academic freedom which the academic community has acknowledged as acceptable within religiously affiliated colleges? Do these limitations allow a college to ground a decision to terminate the employment of a professor solely on the basis of his resignation from a religious community or on the basis of a canonically irregular marriage entered into by the professor? Does it matter whether the professor has already been granted tenure? What procedures should normally apply in a dispute over failure to promote or over termination of a professor's services? These are some of the many questions which have emerged both within the formal public sector of legal dispute resolution by the courts and within the informal private sector in which accrediting agencies and professional associations play a significant role.

B. Legal Analysis

1. Eligibility for public institutional assistance

The first question facing college administrators wishing to assert influence or control over the content of the educational experience is whether attempts to protect the religious character of the institution in this way would render the institution ineligible for public financial assistance. As we saw in chapter four, the Supreme Court trilogy did not address this kind of question directly, but it did intimate that the basis for allowing public assistance to flow to some religiously affiliated colleges is that they are generally characterized by a high degree of respect for principles of academic freedom. Once again, it is significant that the Court has repeatedly invalidated institutional aid to church related elementary and secondary schools while allowing such aid to religiously affiliated colleges and universities, in part on the theory that academic freedom prevails in institutions of higher education but not at the level of elementary and secondary education.

In *Tilton*, for example, Chief Justice Burger noted that the parties had stipulated that "courses at these institutions are taught according to the academic requirements intrinsic to the subject matter and the individual teacher's concept of professional standards" and that there was reliable evidence that "the schools were characterized by an atmosphere of academic freedom rather than religious indoctrination."[6] Burger reached this conclusion in spite of evidence in the form of "several institutional documents that stated certain religious restrictions on what could be taught." He did so evidently because "other evidence showed that these restrictions were not in fact enforced."[7] Finally, he noted that all four colleges involved in *Tilton* "subscribe to the 1940 Statement of Principles on Academic Freedom and Tenure endorsed by the American Association of University Professors and the Association of American Colleges."[8]

The issue of academic freedom was dealt with obliquely by the Court in the other two cases involving public assistance to church related colleges. In *Hunt* Justice Powell alluded to the alleged religious restrictions on course content presented in *Tilton* but dismissed them as permissible "institutional rhetoric."[9] And in *Roemer* Justice Blackmun wrote that nontheology courses at the four Maryland colleges "are taught in an 'atmosphere of intellectual freedom' and without 'religious pressures'" and that as in *Tilton* "[e]ach college subscribes to, and abides by, the 1940 Statement of Principles on Academic Freedom of the American Association of University Professors."[10] Blackmun also observed in a footnote:

> The District Court did not make the same finding with respect to theology and religion courses taught at the appellee colleges. It made no contrary finding, but simply was "unable to characterize the course offerings in these subjects." There was a "possibility" that "these courses could be devoted to deepening religious experiences in the particular faith rather than to teaching theology as an academic discipline." The court considered this possibility sufficient to require that the Council for Higher Education take steps to insure that no public funds would be used to support religion and theology programs.[11]

Justice Stewart dissented from the judgment of the Court and urged as a reason for his dissent a "decisive difference" between *Tilton*, where "the Court emphasized that the theology courses were taught as academic subjects" and *Roemer*, where "the District Court was unable to find that the compulsory religious courses were taught as an academic discipline."[12]

One general conclusion and two particular conclusions emerge from these three decisions. First, the Supreme Court has chosen not to define with particularity the specific elements of academic freedom which it would view as a prerequisite for eligibility for public assistance. Instead it has referred to the policy statement on academic freedom adopted by the Association of American Colleges and the American Association of University Professors in 1940. Hence college administrators must look to this professional standard as a touchstone for resolving the issue of public funding. If their institutions measure up to this standard, they will probably have no difficulty qualifying for public assistance.

Secondly, one may also glean from these cases not simply

a generalized reference to the AAC–AAUP statement, but also a couple of particularized examples of what the Courts will allow. Some measure of "institutional rhetoric" in college and university bulletins describing the general religious orientation of the institution appears to be acceptable, because the Court apparently does not believe that this sort of rhetoric describes the reality of what goes on in the classroom. A different conclusion would undoubtedly have been obtained if the Court were presented with a case of overt and pervasive religious indoctrination.

Thirdly, the Court has intimated that a religiously affiliated college would not be jeopardizing its eligibility for receiving public aid merely by requiring that its students satisfy a requirement of participation in a minimum number of courses in theology or religious studies. This seems clearly to be the case when the required courses are "taught according to the academic requirements of the subject matter and the teacher's concept of professional standards."[13] But if there were an attempt to indoctrinate students or to proselytize,"[14] presumably such courses would jeopardize the permissibility of public aid to the institution. It did not hurt the case for the four Connecticut colleges involved in the *Tilton* case that among the courses which students could elect to fulfill their theology requirement were courses in Judaism and in religious matters ranging broadly beyond the denominational tenets of the Roman Catholic Church. But this breadth does not appear to us to be constitutionally required.

2. Eligibility of students for public assistance

In the previous chapter we noted that a less restrictive standard may apply in a situation where the benefit to the institution is indirect, or where the emphasis of the aid program is on the student rather than on the institution. For in *Americans United for Separation of Church and State* v. *Blanton*[15] the Supreme Court summarily affirmed a lower court opinion sustaining state tuition grants to students attending religiously affiliated colleges, even though "the evidence adduced established that some, but not all, of the private schools whose students benefited from this program are operated for religious purposes . . . and are admittedly *permeated with the dogma of the sponsoring religious organization.*"[16]

The Court was not presented with the same situation in another case, *Smith* v. *Board of Governors,*[17] where the district court made a finding that a high degree of academic freedom characterized the two religiously affiliated institutions, Belmont Abbey and Pfeiffer College, where students might pay their tuition from funds granted them by the State of North Carolina:

> In general, there is academic freedom in the College [of Belmont Abbey]. The College has adopted the 1940 Statement of Academic Freedom of the American Association of University Professors. The Faculty Handbook emphasizes the freedom of each member of the faculty to seek and impart knowledge, interpret findings and draw conclusions without interference because those conclusions are unacceptable to constituted authority within or without the institution. . . . Each teacher selects his own textbooks. . . . Pfeiffer [College] has adopted the 1940 Statement of Academic Freedom of the American Association of University Professors. Each member of the faculty selects the materials to be used in his course, and there is no evidence that the United Methodist Church or any other religious group has attempted to influence the content of any course or the method by which it is taught.[18]

The Supreme Court summarily affirmed the lower court decision in *Smith.*

What may be concluded from *Blanton* is that some federal district courts may not desire to scrutinize the degree of academic freedom found at a religiously affiliated college where students wish to expend funds derived from a state grant and that the Supreme Court has instructed lower courts to uphold such aid to students even if they choose to attend an institution which is "permeated with the dogma of the sponsoring religious organization."

What may be concluded from *Smith,* however, is that the Supreme Court has also given precedential value to a decision which conditioned the permissibility of student aid upon a finding that the institution attended by those students maintains respect for principles of academic freedom. Even after *Blanton* some federal district courts may give greater weight to the rationale of the *Smith* court and require some minimal respect for academic freedom on a campus before allowing state aid to flow through a student to a religiously affiliated college.[19]

3. Governmental regulation and academic freedom

Leaders in higher education have frequently complained about the increase of governmental regulation of the affairs of the academy.[20] Some scholarly work has been undertaken to explore the possibility of a constitutional defense for these institutions based on freedom of association and on academic freedom.[21] And counsel for at least one religiously affiliated college has in the context of litigation with the federal government asserted such a defense based on academic freedom as a constitutionally protected right.[22] Hence it is important to refer as well to Supreme Court cases on academic freedom which did not arise because of a question involving public aid but out of a general concern with limits on the government in its contacts with the academic world.

The Supreme Court has repeatedly suggested that academic freedom is of fundamental importance in our society, and that it will scrutinize carefully practices which would diminish its value. For example, the Court has set limits to governmental control of curriculum,[23] although without mentioning the talismanic phrase "academic freedom" in those decisions. And the Court has refused to uphold exclusive state control over the process of education,[24] but once again without alluding to academic freedom as the basis for its decisions. The cases in which the Court has made direct use of the notion of academic freedom have involved the right of teachers to be free from excessively broad loyalty oaths,[25] governmental investigations[26] or an intrusive or overbroad invasions of teachers' rights of associational privacy.[27]

In these cases the Supreme Court has never elevated academic freedom to the status of an independent constitutional right,[28] but various justices have made it clear that academic freedom is a fundamental value worthy of judicial protection. For example, in *Sweezy* v. *New Hampshire*[29] Chief Justice Warren stressed the significance of academic freedom:

> The essentiality of freedom in the community of American universities is almost self-evident. No one should underestimate the vital role in a democracy that is played by those who guide and train our youth. To impose any strait jacket upon the intellectual leaders in our colleges and universities would imperil the future of our Nation. No field of education is so thoroughly comprehended by man that new discoveries cannot yet be made. Particularly is that true in the social sciences, where few, if any, principles are accepted as absolutes. Scholarship cannot flourish in an atmosphere of suspicion and distrust. Teachers and students must always remain free to inquire, to study and to evaluate, to gain new maturity and understanding; otherwise our civilization will stagnate and die.[30]

A strong argument can be made in support of the claim that the academic community should be afforded the same sort of constitutional protections as are extended to other associations.[31] By the same token, what may be concluded from the series of academic freedom cases outlined above is that these institutions may have an increasingly successful argument to make based on the distinctive character of the academic community as a "marketplace of ideas."[32]

In short, if institutions of higher education are to employ a constitutional defense to governmental regulation which is perceived as intrusive or as destructive of academic autonomy and integrity, they must first be sure that their own houses are in order by safeguarding principles of academic freedom on their campuses. But how are college administrators to know the content of the elusive phrase "academic freedom"? Neither in public funding cases nor in employment disputes have judges elaborated their own prolix definition of the term. They have instead deferred to various statements concerning academic freedom issued by the American Association of University Professors.[33]

4. Legal instruments and AAUP policy

In accepting these statements as indicative of norms or goals commonly accepted within the academic community, the courts have given to these statements an added dimension of legal significance which college administrators should not overlook. W. Todd Furniss, the director of the Office of Academic Affairs in the American Council of Education, recently suggested that college administrators eliminate from legal documents such as employment contracts and faculty manuals or documents with potential legal significance such as bulletins and catalogues, any language which might be construed as binding the institution to the AAUP statements.[34] Ralph Brown and Matthew Finkin, two prominent law professors, responded to the Furniss article, stating their view that Furniss had misunderstood what the courts are actually doing when they rely on AAUP standards, and that courts should give weight to these standards to the extent that they "represent a body of persuasive professional opinion."[35] Whether an administrator is worried about the legal status of AAUP policies with which he disagrees, or whether he wishes to explore the usefulness of AAUP policies, a careful review of the documents which deal with academic freedom is in order.

The statements of the AAUP concerning both the substantive content of academic freedom and the procedural requirements of academic due process have been gathered together into a single volume.[36] Administrators at religiously affiliated colleges may not be legally bound by requirements of the Free Speech Clause of the First Amendment or the Due Process Clause of the Fourteenth Amendment because these colleges are generally not involved in state action.[37] Nevertheless, these administrators must take seriously the expectations of the academic community concerning the substantive and procedural rights of professors, for the fundamental values underlying these rights are at the core of education itself[38] and of education which is informed by religious commitments.[39] Hence administrators should review the AAUP statements with care and, after appropriate consultation with the faculty, incorporate into the governing statutes and regulations of the institution those aspects of substantive academic freedom and procedural academic due process which seem valuable to adopt.

Summary

Administrators of religiously affiliated colleges may strive to ensure that religious and ethical values[40] are incorporated into the educational experience of their institutions without jeopardizing either institutional assistance or aid to their students. The courts will not find either form of public aid impermissible solely on the basis of a requirement that students be exposed to an explicitly religious worldview. But if a college were to seek to impose upon its faculty or student body a narrow definition of sectarian orthodoxy or orthopraxy,[41] it may have to forego institutional assistance. Once again, the courts will look not to the mere fact that theology or religious studies are offered, but to how these courses are taught. If the courses are "taught according to the academic requirements of the subject matter and the teacher's concept of professional standards" there will be no legal difficulty. But if there is any "attempt to indoctrinate students or to proselytize,"[42] public financial assistance to the institution would be constitutionally impermissible.

Private colleges are not generally involved sufficiently in contacts with the state government to be bound to the procedural requirements imposed on public institutions by the Due Process Clause of the Fourteenth Amendment. Nevertheless administrators at religiously affiliated colleges should review the policies of their institutions carefully to determine whether they conform to commonly accepted norms of substantive academic freedom and of procedural academic due process, as articulated in the 1940 statement of the AAC and the AAUP, and to determine whether they might be improved by incorporating some of the recommendations in this area made by the AAUP in 1958, 1971, and 1976. They should do so because the courts do so in ruling on public funding issues, because the societal values undergirding academic freedom and academic due process are also at the core of educational philosophy, and because their religious heritage prompts them to provide moral leadership in promoting the dignity of the human person and in protecting accuracy and openness in the search for truth.

6 Student Admissions and Student Discipline

A. The Practice of Religious Preference in Student Admissions and Religious Influence in Student Discipline

AS WE OBSERVED in chapter four, the variety of relationships between church and campus produces a wide range of employment policies. This observation may be extended also to the policies of religiously affiliated colleges concerning the admission of students to the colleges and the discipline expected of or imposed on students while attending these colleges.

Once again, our general assumption is that where there is a strong bond between church and campus, there would probably be a corresponding strong impulse to prefer students who are members of the sponsoring religious body or at least to recruit actively for such students from the local congregations of that denomination or from the "feeder high schools" associated with that religious community. We also assume that where there is a strong link with a sponsoring religious body, there is generally a greater tendency to enforce the moral teaching of the church than there would be without a strong link to a church or religious body.

1. Student admissions

The survey of administrators of religiously affiliated colleges did not yield sufficient data to confirm or to negate these assumptions, but we did gather some information which may be useful for further research in this area. Of those expressing an opinion concerning the ability of religiously affiliated colleges to exercise religious preference in selection of their student bodies without thereby forfeiting their entitlement to receipt of public benefits, 71.8 percent expressed agreement and 28.2 percent expressed disagreement. When, however, these institutions were asked whether as a matter of practice they exercised such religious preference, only 29.1 percent indicated that they did and 70.9 percent indicated that they did not. And when asked to identify an approximate percentage of their student bodies who are members of the religious body or church to which the college is affiliated, 10 percent responded that this information was unavailable. The median average percent of students who are members of the religious body affiliated with responding colleges was 53.7 percent.

2. Student discipline

When asked whether their institutions maintain a policy of disciplining students for failure to conform to a code of ethical conduct or of religious beliefs, 64.4 percent responded in the affirmative and 27.5 percent responded in the negative. Among the specific areas of ethical concerns or religious beliefs manifested in these kinds of codes of student discipline are the following items, listed in order of frequency of appearance in the respondents' answers: prohibition against use of unlawful drugs (63.7 percent), prohibition against extramarital sex (43.1 percent), prohibition against drinking alcoholic beverages (41.2 percent), required attendance at religious services or compulsory chapel rule (22.5 percent), prohibition against smoking or use of tobacco (16.9 percent), and prohibition against dancing (15 percent). Of our respondents 46.9 percent reported that there was cause to enforce these sorts of ethical provisions in codes of student discipline within the past five academic years (1973–1978) and that the sanctions for violations ranged from counseling guidance to suspension and expulsion.

3. Student aid and governmental regulation

One other piece of information gathered in our survey is significant for the legal analysis relating to the permissibility of religious preference in student admissions policies. Although 13.1 percent of the respondents to our survey indicated that as a matter of policy they do not accept institutional assistance from the federal government, all of these respondents acknowledged that students who attend their institutions receive some form of federal assistance. This finding confirms the data in a 1976 survey among the constituency of the American Association of Presidents of Independent Colleges and Universities, in which all but 2 of 85 respondents (97.7 percent) indicated that their students received some form of public assistance.[1]

Congress has considerable constitutional authority to regulate under both the Taxing and Spending Power (Art. I, Sec. 8, Cl. 1) and the Commerce Clause Power (Art. I, Sec. 8, Cl. 3). After the famous shift in the Supreme Court in 1937 away from the invalidation of the New Deal, the Court has regarded these powers as "plenary" and has almost invariably upheld social legislation enacted under these constitutional grants of authority.[2] Hence when Congress wished to enact the historic Civil Rights Act of 1964, it relied in part on the Commerce Clause as its constitutional warrant for the legislation.[3] And when it subsequently enacted other civil rights legislation, it relied in part on the Taxing and Spending Power to proscribe discrimination on the basis of sex and of handicap in federally funded programs.[4]

To state that the federal powers to enact civil rights legislation are broad is not to say that they are limitless. All attempts by the federal government to regulate under these powers are subject, of course, to other constraints imposed by the Constitution. For example, the government may not compel a person to forgo his Fifth Amendment right against self-incrimination by requiring incriminating declarations on tax forms.[5] Nor may it, in keeping with the limitations on federal power under the Tenth Amendment, enact legislation under the Commerce Clause setting a minimum wage for state employees.[6]

By the same token, Congress would violate the Free Exercise Clause of the First Amendment if it were to attach to an appropriations bill that provided aid to religiously affiliated colleges, or to students attending them, various conditions which struck at the heart of the religious mission of these institutions. An example of such an unconstitutional regulation would be a federal prohibition on religious preference in policies governing student admissions and student aid at religiously affiliated colleges, or on religious influence in policies concerning student discipline at these colleges. No such prohibition exists in federal legislation concerning student admissions. And to the best of our knowledge, there have not been many instances of conflicts with the federal government arising from an attempt by a federal official to interfere with the right of a religiously affiliated college to maintain a code of student discipline consistent with the ethical standards or precepts of the religious body with which the college is affiliated.[7] If Congress should ever contemplate enacting legislation or if federal agencies should ever contemplate enacting administrative regulations which would have the effect of diminishing the ability of religiously affiliated colleges to carry out their religious mission through policies concerning student admissions and student discipline, administrators at these colleges should be prepared to resist this sort of legislation or regulation as violative of their First Amendment rights.

4. A rationale for religious preference in student admissions

This example is critical for religiously affiliated colleges not because many of them in fact exercise religious preference in choosing their students, for our survey indicates that most do not. It is rather the point that the government has no business telling such institutions that they cannot exercise this kind of religious preference if they choose to do so. This point is made all the more forceful by the fact that many small religiously affiliated colleges have experienced declining enrollment in the past decades and several, as a consequence, have had to close their doors permanently.

Despite these harsh realities, however, there remain many administrators at religiously affiliated colleges who have resisted the impulse to survive by broadening the base of their student body significantly beyond the membership of the church to which the college is connected. These administrators have preferred to assert their religious distinctiveness as a more significant value than the success of the institution measured in terms of the size of its student body. For example, the acting director of research and institutional studies at Valparaiso University, Gary A. Greinke, recently recommended that Lutheran colleges should maintain their prevailing admissions standards giving preference to Lutheran students, even if this policy would have the effect of decreasing enrollment at these institutions in the late 1970s. In his update of Francis C. Gamelin's 1970 study of Lutheran colleges and universities,[8] Dr. Greinke asserted:

> It is necessary for a college to maintain its reputation and sense of mission and this should not be sacrificed for numbers of students. Limiting enrollments consistent with institutional mission will allow an institution to maintain a distinctive purpose.
>
> Some institutions already have a limited Lutheran enrollment. In fact, in some cases, Lutherans are a relatively small minority. Apparently some institutions view their Lutheran affiliation as nominal. The data suggest there are a number of institutions which have from 30 to 60% Lutheran students. These institutions are at a critical juncture in their history. If Lutheran affiliation is to permeate the lifeblood of an institution, it will be necessary to retain a solid core of Lutheran students. . . .

> While non-Lutherans should never feel excluded on a campus, nevertheless, the Lutheran spirit of scholarship, inquiry, and quest for moral and social implications of issues should never be compromised. If an institution is to be distinctive and unique, it must foster and support essential characteristics which make it unique.[9]

No generalization can be made about the religious character of students enrolled at religiously affiliated colleges. Rather, it is for each denomination engaged in higher education and, more locally still, for each religiously affiliated institution of higher education to determine whether and how it wishes to exercise religious preference in the selection of those who make up its student body and whether it chooses to transmit a system of religious and ethical values through a code of student discipline.

B. Legal Analysis

1. Eligibility for public institutional assistance

As was stated above in chapters four and five, the Supreme Court has referred to the employment policies and to the degree of academic freedom present within religiously affiliated colleges in cases concerning the eligibility of these institutions to receive public financial assistance. In the same cases the Court has also made reference to the religious composition of the student body as an element to be factored into the public funding equation. In our opinion, however, the assertions made by various justices of the Supreme Court and other federal judges cannot be regarded as definitive judicial resolutions of the matter of religious preference in student admissions, for these formulations are often vague and contradictory. Although these dicta hardly amount to clear standards, they merit the consideration of college administrators if only because the casualness of these dicta suggests that more reflection must be given to this subject than the justices were prepared to give in the leading public funding cases.

In *Tilton* the Court rejected the appellants' contention that the constitutionality of federal construction grants to religiously affiliated colleges should be decided on the basis of a "composite profile" of the "typical sectarian" institution of higher education. Within the profile argued by the appellants was the imposition of "religious restrictions on admissions."[10] Chief Justice Burger insisted, however, that the Court should focus on actual cases rather than on a hypothetical profile. On this analysis, he wrote that although the "student bodies at each [of the four colleges] are predominantly Catholic, . . . the evidence shows that non-Catholics were admitted as students. . . ."[11] It is difficult to assess what weight this allusion to student admissions had in deciding whether federal construction grants to religiously affiliated colleges would create excessive entanglement between church and state and thus violate one of the Court's standards for adjudication of cases under the Establishment Clause. But presumably one of the ways in which religiously affiliated colleges may avoid being labeled as "pervasively sectarian" is to maintain a policy of admitting at least some (the *Tilton* plurality did not intimate how many) students of a different faith or ecclesial affiliation than that of the sponsoring body.

It should also be noted that Justice White, who has been one of the most forceful proponents of acceptable accommodation in church-state litigation,[12] concurred in the judgment of the Court in *Tilton* but wrote a separate opinion which indicated that he would strike down legislation benefiting religiously affiliated schools on a showing that any of these schools "restricted entry on racial or religious grounds."[13] Although no other justice joined White in this opinion, it appears to have been accepted by some educators as the statement of a minimal standard for eligibility for public assistance,[14] perhaps because Justice White provided the fifth vote in favor of the religiously affiliated colleges involved in *Tilton.*

In *Hunt* the Court upheld the constitutionality of public assistance to the Baptist College at Charleston, South Carolina "despite some institutional rhetoric"[15] about its Christian character. Justice Powell added tersely:

> What little there is in the record concerning the College establishes that there are *no religious qualifications for . . . student admission,* and that only 60% of the College student body is Baptist, a percentage roughly equivalent to the percentage of Baptists in that area of South Carolina. . . .[16]

The language of the "test"—if the term may be used lightly to include this kind of vague assertion—is tighter in *Hunt* than in *Tilton.* In *Tilton* the Court spoke only of the admission of some non-Catholic students to a Catholic college, while in *Hunt* the Court noted that the Baptist college had no religious qualifications for student admission and in fact admitted a percentage of non-Baptists roughly corresponding to the percentage of non-Baptists in the area of the college. Justice Powell concluded: "On the record in this case there is no basis to conclude that the College's operations are oriented significantly towards sectarian rather than secular education."[17]

In *Roemer* the Supreme Court sustained the finding of the district court that the four Roman Catholic colleges in question were not so "pervasively sectarian" that noncategorical grants to them would run afoul of the Establishment Clause. Justice Blackmun's plurality opinion[18] noted that this conclusion was supported by a "number of subsidiary findings concerning the role of religion on these campuses."[19] Among such findings was the following:

> The great majority of students at each of the colleges are Roman Catholic, but the District Court concluded from a "thorough analysis of the student admission and recruiting

> criteria" that the student bodies "are chosen without regard to religion."[20]

According to Justice Blackmun, then, a court reviewing a scheme of financial assistance to a religiously affiliated college might and perhaps should scrutinize the college's recruitment policies. And Blackmun even seems to assert that for such a college to remain eligible for public funding, it must choose its student body on a policy which is religiously nondiscriminatory. It is scant comfort to many a church related college that Justice Blackmun allows that the mere fact that a majority of its student body are adherents to the faith of the sponsoring religious body would not yield the conclusion that the institution is "pervasively sectarian."

In sum, a coherent federal policy on religious preference in student admissions can hardly be discerned from the three cases cited above. Justice White seemed totally opposed to such preference in *Tilton,* while Chief Justice Burger and three other justices seemed to think some such preference was permissible, but did not choose to state how much would be allowable before a judicial boom might be lowered on the authority of the Establishment Clause. Justice Powell in *Hunt* highlighted the fact that the colleges involved in that case maintained "no religious qualifications for student admissions" (similar to Justice White's standard) but encumbered his "test" with a bewildering mathematical component by noting that "only 60% of the College student body is Baptist, a percentage roughly equivalent to the percentage of Baptists in that area of South Carolina." And in *Roemer* Justice Blackmun appears also to agree with Justice White when he makes something, if not much, of the lower court finding that the student bodies "are chosen without regard to religion." Of the four "tests"—if they were ever intended by their authors as such—which are inferable from these dicta, Chief Justice Burger's is probably the best in that it at least allows religiously affiliated colleges to choose some of their students on the basis of religion. In our opinion, however, none of these dicta means that college administrators are constitutionally compelled to eliminate religious preference from their admissions policies if they wish their colleges to remain eligible for public institutional assistance.

2. Eligibility of students for public assistance

As we saw in chapters four and five, the Supreme Court recently affirmed two cases upholding state aid made available to students attending religiously affiliated colleges. In the *Blanton* case the lower federal court made a finding that "some, but not all of the private schools whose students benefited from the program are operated . . . with religious requirements for students. . . ."[21] Although it is impossible to tell from the court's opinion whether the "religious requirements for students" referred to a policy of student admission or student discipline, this distinction did not seem to be crucial to the court, for it did not elaborate further on the statement and it sustained the student aid in question.

In the companion case, *Smith* v. *Board of Governors,* the Supreme Court summarily affirmed a lower court ruling which sustained a state tuition grant program where students attending religiously affiliated colleges were predominantly members of the sponsoring church.[22] Among the facts which the district court chose to highlight was the fact that Belmont Abbey College (Catholic affiliated) does not inquire about the religious affiliation or preference of student applicants.[23] But such a policy is surely not legally necessary, for the court also upheld grants to students attending Pfeiffer College (Methodist affiliated) where there is "extensive use of Methodist ministers in recruiting students."[24] The court noted further that 47 percent of the students receiving scholarships granted by Belmont Abbey College were non-Catholics.[25] Once again, though, the court drew no legal conclusion from this policy, for it noted that "some of Pfeiffer's privately established scholarship funds were established by Methodists, some of which impose religious restrictions upon the selection of recipients."[26]

From *Blanton* and *Smith,* we conclude that administrators of religiously affiliated colleges would not jeopardize the eligibility of students attending these institutions to receive public financial assistance by any of the following policies: (1) exercising religious preference in student admissions, (2) maintaining religious influence in a code of student discipline, (3) having ministers of the religious body with which the college is affiliated recruit for students, or (4) administering scholarship funds restricted to members of a particular religion.

3. Eligibility for tax benefits

The tax-exempt status of a college is a significant tax benefit because it undoubtedly has the effect of increasing private donations to the institution by way of corresponding tax benefits to donors. In determining the eligibility of a college for tax-exempt status under section 501 (c) (3) of the Internal Revenue Code, neither Congress nor the Internal Revenue Service has ever so much as intimated that they have any reservations about the legitimacy and propriety of religious preference in the selection of students at religiously affiliated educational institutions. As was mentioned above in chapter four, according to existing federal tax policy, a religiously affiliated college may exercise religious preference in faculty employment without jeopardizing its tax-exempt status. Similarly, the Internal Revenue Service has not issued any ruling or regulation which would question the tax-exempt status of a college which openly practiced religious preference of students who are members of the religious body sponsoring the college.

Until most recently the rulings issued by the Internal Revenue Service concerning loss of tax-exempt status because of an institutional policy which is discriminatory have been limited to discrimination on the basis of *race*.[27] The chief concern reflected in these rulings and regulations has been that a private school established to undermine the effect of the Court's teaching in *Brown* v. *Board of Education* should not do so with the assistance of the federal tax policy.[28] The tax-exempt status of a church related college would be placed in question only by a student admissions policy which, although nominally limited to religious preference, had the actual effect of racial discrimination. Indeed after recent decisions by the Supreme Court concerning civil rights, it would seem that the tax-exempt status of an institution could be removed by the IRS only if there was evidence of a deliberate intent[29] to discriminate on the basis of race.

According to recent IRS guidelines on the availability of tax-exempt status for schools maintained by a religious body, the IRS will not allow such a school to bolster a racially discriminatory policy on the ground that "a tenet of the religion which it embraces requires that the schools maintain [such] a . . . policy. . . ."[30] Although the Supreme Court has declined to rule on the precise question of whether religiously motivated racial discrimination may derive some constitutional succor from the Free Exercise Clause,[31] the Court has clearly affirmed the power of the IRS to deny the tax benefit of being classed as a charitable organization to schools which practice racial discrimination.[32]

On November 16, 1977, the IRS issued two private letter rulings[33] concerning scholarship funds restricted in one instance to members of a particular religion[34] and in the other case to male students.[35] The IRS indicated that neither discrimination on the basis of religion nor gender-based discriminiation of this sort offended against the federal tax policy and that a donor making a gift with such restrictions could take advantage of the tax benefits provided for charitable donations in the Internal Revenue Code.

In summary, neither Congress nor the Internal Revenue Service has ever denied the legitimacy of a policy of religious preference in student admissions by a school which is religiously affiliated. To the contrary, the IRS recently issued an opinion that scholarship funds restricted to students who are members of a particular religion may qualify as tax-deductible charitable contributions. If, however, religious preference in student admissions were merely a cloak to cover over a policy of intentional racial discrimination by a school, the IRS would be bound by existing precedents to withdraw the tax-exempt status of that institution. Although the Supreme Court has not yet ruled definitively on the question of whether the Free Exercise Clause protects assertions of a religious motivation for racial discrimination, the IRS has refused to allow such a defense to be raised by church supported schools which maintain an intentional policy of racial discrimination.

4. Student discipline

Our research has not uncovered any cases in which a federal court has ruled that a religiously affiliated college would be ineligible for public financial assistance if it maintained a policy of disciplining students for failure to conform to ethical standards imposed by the college.[36] And the deferential attitude of the Supreme Court toward administrators of public institutions of higher education suggests that the Court would not be willing to impose stricter requirements on administrators of religiously affiliated colleges.[37]

On the other hand, if religiously affiliated colleges maintain a policy of disciplining students for failure to comply with religious practices such as compulsory chapel attendance,[38] it is our opinion that they will undoubtedly risk not only the loss of eligibility of their institutions for receipt of public institutional assistance but also the loss of their students' eligibility for student aid. This conclusion is based not only on dicta in the Supreme Court's trilogy of cases on public funding,[39] but also on the square holding of at least one lower federal court that state tuition aid could not flow to students attending a religiously affiliated college with a compulsory chapel requirement,[40] and on the general reluctance of the courts to allow any form of coercion of religious practices.[41]

5. State law governing student admissions policies

In chapter four we saw that there is no consistency between the federal civil rights statutes and the statutes of the several states concerning religious preference in the employment policies of religious corporations, associations, or societies. This inconsistency is replicated in the area of state laws governing student admissions policies. To illustrate this point, we include here two patterns of state statutes in this area as examples of the wide variety of legal restraints imposed by states on the exercise of religious preference in student admissions.

As was mentioned in chapter four, some states have enacted the Model Anti-Discrimination Act prepared by the National Commission on Uniform State Laws. Section 502 of this Act contains a general prohibition of religiously based discrimination against any student seeking admission. In section 503 (1) the Model Act provides that it is not a discriminatory practice for:

> A religious educational institution or an educational institution operated, supervised, or controlled by a religious institution or organization to limit admission or give preference to applicants of the *same religion;*[42]

Five states have enacted statutes containing language similar to this provision, but each state has added some changes.[43]

For example, the New York statute contains the following general statement of policy:

> It is hereby declared to be the policy of the state that the American ideal of equality of opportunity requires that students, otherwise qualified, be admitted to educational institutions without regard to race, color, religion, creed or national origin, except that, with regard to religious or denominational educational institutions, students, otherwise qualified, shall have the equal opportunity to attend therein without discrimination because of race, creed, color or national origin. It is a fundamental American right for members of various religious faiths to establish and maintain educational institutions exclusively or primarily for students of their own religious faith or to effectuate the religious principles in furtherance of which they are maintained. Nothing herein contained shall impair or abridge that right. . . .[44]

The statute defines a religious or denominational educational institutions as:

> an educational institution which is operated, supervised or controlled by a religious or denominational organization and which has certified to the state commissioner of education, that it is a religious or denominational educational institution.[45]

And it repeats the grant to such institutions of an explicit exemption from the general prohibition against religious preference in student selection:

> . . . nothing in this section shall be deemed to affect, in any way, the right of a religious or denominational educational institution to select its students exclusively or primarily from members of such religion or denomination or from giving preference in such selection to such members or to make such selection of its students as is calculated by such institution to promote the religious principles for which it is established or maintained.[46]

According to the plain meaning of the Model Act, a Catholic college would be guilty of an unfair educational practice if it were to exercise preference for members of any other faith than the Catholic faith. New York has broadened this provision, enabling any religiously affiliated school to exercise whatever religious preference in student selection it deems to be consistent with its religious principles. Because there is no uniformity among the several states in their laws governing student admissions policies at nonpublic colleges we repeat the recommendation given above in chapter four. College administrators need the advice of counsel familiar with state and municipal law which might apply to their student admissions policies.

7 Use of Publicly Funded Facilities

When religiously affiliated colleges and universities receive public funds in the form of grants or loans to construct campus facilities, restrictions inevitably are imposed with respect to the use of these facilities. Legal problems exist with restrictions on use of state[1] as well as federally funded facilities, but for the sake of simplicity and clarity, discussion will be limited to federally funded facilities.

In the Center survey discussed earlier[2] the item most often cited in the survey responses as an example of government interference with the religious mission of the institutions was the limitation on the use of facilities constructed at least in part by federal grants or loans. The two major problems were identified as prohibitions on teaching of courses in religion and theology and on conducting religious services in buildings constructed with federal funds, and these issues were raised by colleges and universities across the country which were affiliated with various denominations and religious orders.

Some measure of the importance of these issues to the colleges can be taken from survey responses which disclosed that ninety-three of the responding institutions received more than $200 million in federal funds over the past fifteen years under the Higher Education Facilities Act as amended. The average amount received by each institution exceeded $2,160,000. These figures are even more striking when it is understood that survey responses included only a handful of the major church related universities which tend to receive much larger amounts of these funds on the average than do the small colleges.[3]

The Higher Education Facilities Act of 1963 was passed by Congress to provide a program of grants and loans to institutions of higher education for construction of academic and related facilities. That act was subsequently amended, but the programs were continued under the new legislation, and the original definition of "academic facilities" was carried through each amendment. It prohibits funding under the act for "any facility used or to be used for sectarian instruction or as a place for religious worship."[4] In addition, there is a further restriction imposed that ". . . no facility constructed, reconstructed or renovated with assistance under this subchapter shall ever be used for religious worship or a sectarian activity or for a school or department of divinity."[5]

The language of these sections seems clear enough, but a multitude of questions have been raised about its application. Is a university permitted to hold annual baccalaureate services in a campus center constructed with federal funds received under this act? Can meetings of student religious organizations be held in rooms of this campus center, or can offices in the center be used by these student religious organizations? What about the use of publicly funded dormitories by students for informal religious worship? Does it make a difference if a campus chaplain is involved? Can the campus chaplain or staff persons from off-campus religious foundations use those dormitory facilities for individual or group counseling? Can they be used for informal discussion groups if religious or theological topics are included?

Can classroom or other facilities constructed with these funds be used for the teaching of religion in any form?

Can these buildings be used as offices of faculty who teach religion, theology, or sacred music?

What about religious symbols on buildings constructed with federal funds? Is there any point at which one such symbol or a combination of them violate the terms of the Act?

If fees are not charged to a group engaged in any "religious" activity for the use of publicly funded facilities, does that imply constitutionally questionable financial support to the group? If fees are charged for use of the facilities, must they be charged uniformly to all groups for all uses? Must the fees be set high enough to cover all expenses incurred?

We find a remarkable lack of clarity in the regulations and case law, which do not offer guidance to college administrators about these issues. Neither a review of the extensive legislative history nor an examination of the regulations cited under this act[6] offers any enlightenment. The loan agreement which merely replicates the statutory restriction provides no further guidance.

We find few cases which interpret these statutory provisions as they apply to church related higher education. However, a dearth of reported court decisions does not mean that a particular regulation or law is not causing problems for the institutions being regulated. Difficult conflicts may not reach formal adjudication; the institutions may simply comply as a result of administrative pressure from HEW representatives. These are important problems which deserve serious attention even if they were not widespread, and as we shall see, both college administrators and government officials are reaching erroneous conclusions about the mandates of the legislation.

We are aware from personal contacts that some HEW officials are prepared to interpret the restrictions in very broad terms indeed, some of which range well beyond the wording of the act. For example, one investigator told officials of a southern college related to the United Methodist Church that the use of a humanities building constructed in part with federal funds for the teaching of sacred music courses and for offices of an instructor who taught courses in religion violated the statute. The official insisted that the Office of Education would call the loan and require the return of grant funds immediately unless the college stopped both of these uses of this building. The college protested that neither the sacred music course nor the courses in religion were taught in any way from a "sectarian" point of view, but in order to avoid the expenses of litigation (which it should have won handily) the college complied with the orders.

The problems posed by this kind of process are twofold: religiously affiliated colleges are being required to comply with interpretations of the law which are at best questionable, and those standards are being established at the lowest levels of administrative regulation, so they may vary considerably among regional offices of HEW or even within those regions according to the personal whims of the investigator.

Judicial Decisions

The United States Supreme Court has provided little guidance in this area, but it is useful to consider the few fragments of the opinions to gather what learning is available for direction in these matters.

Eight years after enactment of the Higher Education Facilities Act the United States Supreme Court decided *Tilton* v. *Richardson,* discussed in prior chapters. Chief Justice Burger, writing for a plurality of the Court, noted that the district court had made findings that none of the four Catholic colleges involved in that litigation had violated the statutory restrictions and added that "there are no religious symbols or plaques in or on" the buildings constructed in part by the funds made available under that act.[7] Since that time, it has been assumed by some observers that the statute thus forbids placing religious symbols on buildings constructed with federal funds.

The matter is only casually mentioned in a subsequent opinion of the Supreme Court. In *Roemer,* Justice Blackmun noted that "some classrooms have religious symbols."[8] And in *Smith* the Supreme Court affirmed the judgment of a three-judge panel in which the judges noted in a *per curiam* opinion that "[i]n several of the buildings [at Belmont Abbey College] there are crucifixes, crosses and other religious art."[9]

In each instance, the treatment of this issue is almost offhanded, and it is difficult to believe that the Court meant to indicate that the Constitution requires a prohibition of the use of religious symbols on these buildings. Furthermore, it does not appear that Congress required such a prohibition, because nowhere in the act itself nor in its legislative history is there any intimation about the desires of Congress on this matter. In all of these cases, of course, the public funding was sustained, and no further guidance about the use of public facilities was provided by the Court.[10]

In addition, the prevailing opinions of the Supreme Court trilogy discussed previously which dealt with the issue of public funding to religiously affiliated colleges concentrated attention upon the integrity of the academic enterprise and the atmosphere of academic freedom of the institutions in question, rather than what the Court appeared to regard as the relatively peripheral matters of structural or formal legal control of a college by the affiliated religious body. There simply is no support for the position which would strain the wording of the statute in urging that activities such as the placing of religious symbols on a building or permitting a religiously oriented student group to use a federally funded facility for a meeting place should be seen to violate the act.[11]

While the Supreme Court touched only tangentially on the issues related to the use of publicly funded property at religiously affiliated colleges, our research discloses no other cases involving the Higher Education Facilities Act. It is necessary, therefore, to attempt to secure guidance from cases in which the focus is turned elsewhere.

In this chapter we do not attempt to provide a comprehensive review of all cases dealing with the use of publicly funded facilities, but only a representative selection which illuminate key principles in this area of the law. It is easy to identify genuine and fundamental differences of judicial opinion in these areas, and those differences underscore the difficulties for administrators of religiously affiliated colleges in determining what standards should be utilized for any particular campus situation. Only two cases emerge from research which treat these questions at the university level, and in each the issue was the use of facilities at a public university campus for religious purposes.

In *Keegan* v. *University of Delaware*[12] the university sought an injunction to enforce a campus regulation which prohibited students and priests from conducting religious worship services in the common room of a student dormitory, claiming that the Establishment Clause of the First Amendment required the banning of all religious services. The students and priests responded that the enforcement of the ban infringed the Free Exercise Clause of the First Amendment. The court observed that this case was unique and that counsel were unable to supply precise precedents for the issues at stake.

The Delaware Supreme Court ruled unanimously that the university could not prohibit the religious services in this fashion. In reaching that decision the court determined that 1) permitting religious worship in the common room of a campus dormitory would not violate the Establishment Clause, because to allow religious groups the same use of the facilities as other groups did not advance religion but was rather a lawful accommodation of religion, 2) the university policy imposed a legally recognizable burden on the defendants' constitutional right to free exercise of their religion, 3) the university had not demonstrated the required "compelling state interest" to justify the burden on free exercise.

The court emphasized that this space in question was not a separate religious facility, but a common area provided for general student use. The case was remanded for an evidenciary hearing to determine if the university could show a compelling interest to justify the ban. After an unsuccessful petition for certiorari to the United States Supreme Court, the university chose not to contest the matter further.

In *Stacy* v. *Williams*[13] student, faculty, and other plaintiffs filed lawsuits attacking the constitutionality of regulations for off-campus speakers imposed by public colleges and universities in Mississippi. The three judge district court reviewed several of the regulations, including one which the court construed as preventing student groups from inviting outside speakers on religious topics. The court stated that the university was not compelled to permit outside religious groups to conduct public worship services on campus, but the court found this rule invalid as it was construed. If it were revised, the court said that it "must specifically be confined to forbidding only religious services conducted on the campus by persons having no connection with the university."[14]

Issues related to the use of public facilities for religious purposes have been raised with far greater frequency at the primary and secondary levels in the public schools.[15] As discussed earlier the United States Supreme Court has distinguished sharply between elementary-secondary and postsecondary education for purposes of determining the constitutionality of public funding. It may be that at some point in the future the Court will continue such a distinction in determining what are permitted uses of publicly funded facilities as well. Until that distinction is made, however, we believe it is instructive to consider judicial decisions in the precollegiate area.

Vivid illustrations of the key questions examined by the courts in such litigation are provided in two recent cases,

Resnick v. *East Brunswick Board of Education*,[16] decided by the New Jersey Supreme Court in 1978, and *Johnson* v. *Huntington Beach Union High School District*,[17] decided by a California appellate court in 1977. Although our discussion is limited to federal constitutional issues in these cases, both courts considered the permissibility of the use of school property in question, under both federal and state constitutions. Both courts were divided. While they are readily distinguishable on their facts, the language of the majority opinion in each case strongly indicates a different judicial attitude about the broader issues involved.

The New Jersey Supreme Court in *Resnick* decided, by a five to two majority, that use of public school facilities for worship by religious groups during noninstructional hours was prohibited by neither state nor federal constitution so long as the use was temporary and the school board's out-of-pocket costs were reimbursed. The court observed that while there is a split among jurisdictions as to whether school premises may be constitutionally used for religious purposes, the only case in the last thirty-five years which addressed the federal constitutional issue upheld its use.[18]

The court undertook a careful survey of the tests promulgated by United States Supreme Court decisions in related areas and concluded that where "essentially no public expense is incurred as a result of a benefit received by religious groups," they should not be precluded from receiving the benefit "on the same terms as to other groups of the same class,"[19] i.e., other nonprofit organizations in this school district. The court concluded that incidental wear and tear on school property was "de minimis" and not a prohibited benefit to the religious group, but they were required to reimburse school boards fully for related out-of-pocket expenses directly attributable to their use, such as extra utility, heating, administrative, and janitorial costs.

Because school premises were not used during regular school hours there was no need of supervision to insure that "no religion seeps into secular instruction,"[20] but the court was anxious to stress that the use of the premises must be "temporary" to avoid the risk that lengthy and continuous use would "implicate the Board in the promotion of religion."[21] The court did not impose a strict time limit to define "temporary," but suggested that the leasing of school premises by one of the congregations for more than five years "is approaching the outer bounds of reasonable time and nearing the point of prohibited entanglement."[22] The court noted that all of the congregations in question were in the process of securing a permanent place of worship.

For the majority, what is required by the First Amendment in these areas is not "hostility or total indifference" toward religion, but "benevolent neutrality." To underline this point, the court cited Chief Justice Burger's opinion in *Walz* v. *Tax Commission:*

> The course of constitutional neutrality in this area cannot be an absolutely straight line; rigidity could well defeat the basic purpose of these provisions, which is to insure that no religion be sponsored or favored, none commanded, and none inhibited. The general principle deducible from the First Amendment and all that has been said by the Court is this: that we will not tolerate either governmentally established religion or governmental interference with religion. Short of those expressly proscribed governmental acts there is room for play in the joints productive of a benevolent neutrality which will permit religious exercise to exist without sponsorship and without interference.[23]

In *Johnson* v. *Huntington Beach Union High School District*[24] the California appellate court ruled by a two to one majority that permitting a voluntary student Bible study club to meet and conduct its activities on the school campus during the school day was prohibited by the Establishment Clauses of both federal and state constitutions. The resulting prohibition was determined to be a permissible infringement of the students' rights under the Free Exercise Clause.

The court observed that "Preservation of religious liberty and maintenance of governmental neutrality have undergone their severest test in the context of religious exercises within school corridors,"[25] and after a review of United States Supreme Court opinions concluded that to permit such student meetings would have the impermissible "primary effect" of advancing religion by granting a "financial subsidy" resulting from the free use of school facilities such as classrooms, heat and light, and by stamping the school district's "imprimatur upon religious activity."[26] Under school district regulations the club would become an entity "sponsored" by the school which would be entitled to use the school's name in connection with its activities and thus become a part of the school's extracurricular program during the school day (lunch hours) when the students were compelled by law to attend school.

In addition, the court stated that excessive state entanglement would necessarily result from the state statutory requirements that the school supply a faculty advisor who must attend all club functions and approve all club activities, and that the school would have to audit club financial accounts and review membership procedures to insure that they were neither secret nor discriminatory.

All of these cases are illustrative of the range of complex issues connected with the use of publicly funded facilities at religiously affiliated colleges, though none is really on point. It is useful, however, to review in general terms some of the principles enunciated in these opinions to elicit some guidance for college administrators who must make decisions in this area on a regular basis, and to assist in predicting the probable outcome of litigation which will surely arise sooner or later concerning the legitimacy of various uses of publicly funded facilities at religiously affiliated colleges.

1. Uniformity of treatment

Keegan may not be a case directly on point for our purposes, for it involved a public university, but it is certainly the closest of kin out of all the cases reviewed. The thrust of that opinion was to permit religious groups access to publicly owned facilities on the same basis as they are made available to other similar groups, even if the activities in question included worship services. *Resnick* strongly echoed the *Keegan* court on this point. Uniformity of treatment has emerged as a sound principle of constitutional law.[27]

2. Public subsidy of religious activity

It is generally agreed in these cases that religious organizations and activities should not receive any significant subsidy from public funds. The *Resnick* majority spelled out in detail what services must be paid for by the church groups as out-of-pocket expenses and determined that incidental wear and tear on the school property in question was a permissible "de minimis" benefit to a religious group when other nonprofit groups received the same benefits.[28]

In *Keegan* there was no discussion of what expenses were involved with the use of the common room of the dormitory. It seems probable as a factual matter that there were few if any expenses involved. It may be, however, that the *Keegan* court would simply say that the critical question is uniformity of treatment with other groups, and any "subsidy" which the university provided to other campus groups in terms of utilities or janitorial services would have to be extended as well to religious groups.

It is hard to imagine the *Johnson* majority would agree, for it viewed the rent-free use of classroom space to a Bible study group as impermissible financial aid of a religious group.

3. "Imprimatur" or government approval

The *Johnson* majority was also worried that the Bible study club, under regulations of the school district, would be entitled to use its name and become a part of the extracurricular program of the school in an unacceptable fashion, i.e., become "sponsored" by the school. The dissenting judge disagreed that sponsorship was implied by what he viewed as mere "recognition" of school clubs. These differences in terminology used by the judges to describe the relationship of school to student clubs may serve to emphasize important differences between higher education institutions and primary and secondary schools which were relied upon by the United States Supreme Court in the trilogy of opinions dealing with public funding of religiously affiliated colleges discussed in chapters three and four. The assumptions of Chief Justice Burger in *Tilton* were that church related colleges are attended by more mature students with greater independence of thought than at primary and secondary schools, and the colleges themselves are "characterized by a higher degree of academic freedom and seek to evoke free and critical responses from their students."[29]

At virtually all colleges and universities in this nation, student groups and activities operate with a far greater degree of freedom and autonomy than is characteristic of students at primary and secondary schools. This emphasis on the fundamental importance of the freedom of students to be organized and active in groups and causes with which the university may not agree has been reaffirmed in recent decisions by federal courts and the United States Supreme Court involving public universities.[30] The Supreme Court underlined the place of the campus as "peculiarly" the "marketplace of ideas" and emphasized the importance of access to campus facilities "for meetings and other appropriate purposes" for the constitutionally protected exercise of the freedoms of speech and association by campus organizations.[31]

The federal court in *Stacy* v. *Williams* pointed out that if a college or university wishes to do so, it may require that a statement be made at campus meetings and events that the views presented by speakers or groups do not necessarily represent those of the institution.[32] This technique has been encouraged by the United States Supreme Court in other contexts. In 1951 the Court first suggested that where there are "reasonable and adequate alternatives" to enforcement of a public policy, the government should avail itself of those alternatives rather than burden the exercise of commercial rights protected by the Constitution.[33] The "least restrictive alternative" doctrine has subsequently been applied to cases involving First Amendment rights,[34] and it seems wholly applicable to speeches and other gatherings on the campus.

Each of these elements is individually significant: 1) the distinction between institutions of higher education and primary and secondary schools, 2) the fundamental importance of preserving the university as an open "marketplace of ideas," and 3) the ease with which the university can make clear that allowing speeches and other activities or recognizing campus groups does not necessarily imply approval of the message or the purposes thereof. Taken together, these factors render the concern of the *Johnson* majority about the potential "imprimatur" effect of permitting religious activities inapplicable in the context of a college or university campus.

4. Tension between Free Exercise and Establishment Clauses

The tension between the opposing thrusts of the Free Exercise and Establishment Clauses has been widely recognized. The United States Supreme Court has called this internal conflict within the First Amendment Religion Clauses a "paradox."[35] In the view of many legal scholars, in the event of a clash between the Religion Clauses of the First Amendment, the Free Exercise Clause should occupy the place of supremacy; these scholars have accordingly criticized the Court for allowing the Free Exercise Clause to be eclipsed by the Establishment Clause in recent First Amendment litigation.[36] In any event, the conflict between competing claims raised under these two clauses continues to create legal uncertainty. For purposes of illustration, we need not undertake a review beyond the cases already discussed in this chapter.

In *Keegan* the court specifically determined that the Establishment Clause was not violated by permitting the worship services to be held in the dormitory, and that the university's prohibition of those services violated the free exercise rights of the students. The *Resnick* majority accepted the concept of the dominance of the Free Exercise Clause, but concluded that the question of the propriety of permitting church groups to use school premises was not a free exercise question. It was rather a question of whether permitting the use on a uniform basis with other similar groups ran afoul of the Establishment Clause, and because the government stance was that of "benevolent neutrality," there was no violation. In *Johnson,* by contrast, the majority detected substantial violations of the Establishment Clause in the use of school premises by the student Bible club, and only a limited and acceptable limitation on the free exercise rights of the students.

As indicated earlier it is not necessarily possible to unravel consistent strands of analysis from these opinions, but as stated in the opinions themselves the analysis must reach beyond "catch phrases" to examine the factual context carefully[37] and then make judgments which must necessarily be matters of degree.[38] The uncertain patterns of the applicable legal standards may seem surprising, but a comprehensive examination of these legal patterns is vital to an appreciation of current problems for administrators of religiously affiliated colleges in deciding what standards apply to use of publicly funded property at the college.

Conclusion

As has been apparent throughout this volume, it is often the task of an attorney for a religiously affiliated college to offer advice based upon legal sources which are less than certain. This area is no exception, but we venture to offer some specific suggestions based upon our reading of the statute and scattered cases which appear to be relevant. It must be clearly understood, however, that government administrators may not agree with these interpretations, so that as in other areas, a college may be required to undertake litigation to establish its position in these matters.

1. Academic activities which meet the standards of the Supreme Court trilogy for determining the propriety of public funding should be permissible in facilities funded under this statute. For example, the teaching of philosophy of religion or sacred music with academic integrity should not be viewed as "sectarian instruction." Neither should there be a prohibition on the use of the facilities in question for offices by faculty who teach these kinds of courses.

The United States Supreme Court has recognized the importance of the study and understanding of religion:

> It might well be said that one's education is not complete without a study of comparative religion or the history of religion and its relationship to the advancement of civilization. It certainly may be said that the Bible is worthy of study for its literary and historic qualities. Nothing we have said here indicates that such study of the Bible or of religion, when presented objectively as part of a secular program of education, may not be effected consistently with the First Amendment.[39]

College administrators should not allow government officials to impose an unreasonably restrictive definition upon the statutory wording or to limit unduly the use of these premises for legitimate and important academic activity.

2. In addition, the use of these facilities for other gatherings or assemblies should not be restricted unless they are indeed "religious worship" or "sectarian activity" or "sectarian instruction." For example, meetings of campus religious organizations and counseling sessions with clergy are ordinarily neither worship nor sectarian activity. If the activity is being led by a campus chaplain or if clerical persons are

otherwise involved, that fact may provide evidence about whether this is a "sectarian activity," but it obviously cannot be determinative in and of itself.

3. Finally, and perhaps of greatest practical importance, administrators of religiously affiliated colleges should take advantage of provisions which permit the construction of certain areas within a federally funded facility which would be paid for with private funding and which could then be used for otherwise prohibited activities such as worship or sectarian instruction. Frequently respondents to the Center survey indicated that they believed they could not use for the prohibited sectarian activities or religious worship any part of a building which was only partially constructed with federal grants and loans. Other administrators of religiously affiliated colleges were able to work out agreements with HEW officials which permit them to use for chapel services or Mass, for example, portions of the building which were built with private funds.

There appears to be clear authority for this process in the statute:

> If . . . (2) the facility ceases to be used as an academic facility, or the facility is used as a facility excluded from the term "academic facility", unless the Secretary determines that there is good cause for releasing the institution from its obligation, the United States shall be entitled to recover from such applicant (or successor) an amount which bears to the then value of the facility (or so much thereof as constituted an approved project or projects) the same ratio as the amount of such Federal grant or grants bore to the development cost of the facility financed with the aid of such grant or grants. Such value shall be determined by agreement of the parties or by action brought to the United States district court for the district in which such facility is situated.[40]

This section apparently permits the portion of a building funded by college or other private resources to be used for purposes other than those permitted by the statute. In addition, the thrust of this section implies a far greater degree of flexibility in negotiating about these matters than is often exhibited by HEW officials empowered to construe the act in the first instance. These officials may demand summarily an immediate return of grant funds or threaten to call any remaining portions of a loan if a recipient is found not to be complying with the often strained interpretation of the official about requirements of the act.

It appears to us that this provision permits negotiations about these matters even though the facility has already been constructed. A college or university seeking to use a portion of some existing federally funded building for a chapel, for example, may be able to do so under this statute, if it uses privately contributed funds to pay the government an amount equal to the proportion of the total cost of the facility which is represented by the portion the college wishes to use for these purposes and, in effect, "buy back" that portion of the building.

8 Property Relationships

IN A TIME of increasing financial pressures some religiously affiliated colleges may be forced to close or merge with another institution or may seek to separate from a relationship with a religious body in order to remove any possible question that the college is qualified to receive public funding.[1] Almost without exception such departures by the college raise questions and sometimes contests about which institution owns what property. These experiences underline the importance of consideration of property ownership questions by campus and religious body alike in order to clarify a common understanding about property holdings and insure that legal documents reflect that understanding.

It is assumed herein that representatives of sponsoring religious bodies and colleges agree that it is important to establish a legal framework which will maintain some degree of security in or control of selected property contributed to the college by or because of the influence of the religious body. It is crucial for all parties to understand prior to the bestowing or arranging for a major gift what the expectations of donor and recipient are with respect to use of the gift. If those expectations and conditions are set forth with the requisite formality, severe problems can be avoided at a later date.

In many instances, of course, there may be great reluctance for college or religious body representatives to raise and discuss these kinds of issues. Representatives of either institution may believe they are in an inferior bargaining position and consequently prefer to leave such matters unresolved rather than risk confrontation which could produce loss of benefits otherwise provided by the continuing ambivalence of the status quo. Or they may simply believe that raising these issues implies a lack of trust of the other parties and will, therefore, be viewed as most impolite or even insulting.

An additional complicating factor which must be kept in mind in many jurisdictions is the involvement of the state attorney general. The role of the attorney general and the courts in the supervision of charitable corporations varies greatly from state to state.[2] The attorney general of Nevada is granted very broad powers over nonprofit corporations chartered within that state.[3] On the other hand, the Michigan statute specifically excludes educational institutions from legislation placing trusts and trustees holding property for charitable purposes under the supervision of the attorney general and the courts.[4] Alabama has no legislation which requires nonprofit corporations to report or render an accounting to any public officials.[5] But even in a state such as Michigan, which limits the power of the attorney general as to trust assets, the attorney general has standing to sue a nonprofit corporation for taking actions which exceed its legal powers.[6] The administrators of colleges and their sponsoring bodies should inform themselves of the various statutes which provide for the supervision of charitable corporations and trusts, and the extent to which such statutes are, in fact, enforced.

As noted in the Introduction, a myriad of legal arrangements exists between religious bodies and colleges. It is ordinarily necessary for the resolution of property ownership questions to look to a) applicable state law, b) legal documents which relate to the property in question, c) the governing documents of the college, and d) even those of the sponsoring religious body.

The property law of the various states differs widely, so this chapter will simply describe some common legal patterns which exist among the states for illustrative purposes. Another variable element in any analysis of this kind is the factual background which raises these property ownership issues. Such questions may arise because the college has fallen on difficult days and is preparing to go out of business and distribute any remaining assets. These issues might be raised because the college administration wishes to dissolve the relationship with the religious body or engage in a course of action which is so unacceptable to the religious body that the religious body may itself wish to sever the relationship and recover property contributed to the college.

Because of this combination of fundamental variables which influences the analysis of property relationships, we will seek to describe in general terms the kinds of issues likely to arise and to suggest some helpful steps to be taken.

We assume for purposes of this section that the religious body does not have voting control of the governing board of the college, nor personal relationships sufficient to influence decisively actions of that board. If that control or influence does exist, the sponsoring religious body usually can dictate property disposition through the college governing board, and this discussion is largely unnecessary. We also assume that under some circumstances the related religious body may seek to recover property which has been contributed to the college not only by it directly but also by others as a result of the relationship of the religious body to the college.

Some Illustrative Questions

The difficulty of these issues can be illustrated by examples which are not at all unusual, but are typical kinds of situations which religious body and college administrators as well as judges have had to face in this nation.

Suppose a gift of $100,000 has been made by an individual donor, who is a long-time and devoted member of a particular religious body, to a college sponsored by that religious body for use in its discretion but "only so long as it is used for Christian higher education purposes." The college administration determines to use this gift as a scholarship endowment, the interest of which is used to provide scholarships to needy students. Ten years after the time the gift is made, the college runs into severe fiscal problems and is forced to close down and dissolve. If this $100,000 fund survives the claims of creditors and the religious body asserts a claim to it, what should a reviewing judge do with that claim?

Should the funds be given over to the religious body to use in its discretion for higher education? Should the funds revert to the donor or his heirs? If there are no other colleges within the court's jurisdiction related to that particular religious body, should the funds be sent to a college in another state which is also related to that same religious body? Or should the court direct the gift to another college related to a different Christian religious body but located within the same county as the original recipient where the judge has jurisdiction (and must run for reelection)?

Are the results the same if the gift was made without express condition only two years prior to the closing of the college in response to persistent solicitation by the president of the college, who promised in writing it would be used only for the purposes specified? Suppose that six weeks after the gift was received with much rejoicing at the college, that particular president retired and the donor, having thus made his peace, proceeded to die intestate, so if the gift reverts to the donor it would go to his ne'er-do-well nephew who intends never to see the inside of church or college.

Suppose instead of dissolving, the college wishes to merge with a neighboring branch of the state university and proposes to the judge that this particular endowment fund would be used to fund scholarships for students at the university who were members of the religious body.

Suppose there had been no specific condition placed by an individual donor on this gift, but it had been made as part of a general campaign among members of the related religious body by the college ten years before, and the campaign promotional literature had indicated clearly that the college was proud of its relationship to the religious body and provided special opportunities of Christian higher education on its campus. Should the answer be different if that campaign had been carried on only two years prior to the closing of the college or its merger with the public institution?

Suppose the donor were the religious body itself and the gifts were made without any express condition, should the gift revert to that religious body to be used as it chooses? Should it revert to the religious body only if the judge is satisfied that it will be immediately redirected to other colleges related to the religious body?

Suppose these questions of ownership of the endowment fund arose not because the college was in financial trouble, but because it resented continued policy intrusions by the religious body and sought to sever the relationship and proclaim itself an institution without connection to any religious body but with a deep concern about teaching values, and it further committed itself to maintain its distinguished department of religion. Suppose instead that the endowment fund ownership question was raised by the sponsoring religious body, which was increasingly dismayed by the recruiting practices of the college, which, while carefully continuing to proclaim its formal relationship to the religious body, exhibited little concern in recruiting students, faculty, or staff who cared about religious or value questions and further was permitting the religion department to disintegrate.

A Lay Person's View—"Fairness"

Again, the exceedingly difficult policy questions are complicated by the fact that the legal answers vary greatly from state to state—not always so much a product of logic as of history and tradition. As a way of approaching that tangle of legal diversity, it may be helpful first to consider a perspective on such problems which might be adopted by an intelligent nonlawyer asked to arbitrate these kinds of issues without reference to legal precedent.

If a lay person were required to render decisions about who should get what property in situations like those just described, the answers would probably be framed in terms of what is "fair" under the circumstances. That, of course, is not easily defined and may well be seen as begging the question, but very often a decision about what is fair in a given situation would be grounded on a judgment about the expectations and commitments for the use of these funds. In the event that something happened to change the circumstances, such as a financial collapse or decision by the college to depart from its relationship with a religious body, what were the expressed intentions of the parties about such change in circumstances? If those intentions were not expressed, would it be possible to determine from surrounding circumstances something about those expectations?

If it were impossible to determine the parties' expectations, or if the evidence seemed foggy or conflicting on that point, where else would our lay arbitrator look in making decisions about a fair outcome? He might want to know certain things: whether the change in circumstances was foreseeable at the time the gift was made; how long after the gift had been made did the change in circumstances come about; whether the gift was made in response to solicitation efforts by the college or the religious body, or at the sole initiative of the donor; what would happen to the property involved if it were taken away from the college?

These are the same kinds of questions with which the courts have grappled under a variety of legal doctrines and labels. This chapter gathers together some of the legal strands for analysis and guidance in planning.

It is useful to discuss separately questions about the distribution of property in instances in which the college seeks to go out of business and dissolve and in instances in which either the college or religious body or both seek to sever the relationship while the college continues in business. In many states the legal answers to these questions are more certain when the college has determined that it can no longer survive and simply seeks to dissolve.

And finally, it is a helpful caution to introduce any such discussion with a comment from a noted scholar in the area: "The law of disposition of property held by non-profit organizations is rather vague."[7]

A. Disposition of Gift Property in the Event of Financial Collapse and Dissolution of the College

1. Model Non-Profit Corporation Act

Ordinarily the first place to look in determining disposition of assets for a college facing collapse is to the nonprofit corporation code of the state in question. Those statutes, as one would expect, vary significantly among the states,[8] but probably the most useful general pattern to examine for illustrative purposes is the Model Non-Profit Corporation Act[9] which has been adopted in its entirety or with amendments, or at least taken into consideration by many state legislatures in the process of enacting a nonprofit corporate code.[10]

The Model Act provides that after satisfying or providing for the liabilities and obligations of the corporation, the following four steps will be followed:

Section 46. Distribution of Assets

b) Assets held by the corporation upon condition requiring return, transfer or conveyance, which condition occurs by reason of the dissolution, shall be returned, transferred or conveyed in accordance with such requirements;

c) Assets received and held by the corporation subject to limitations permitting their use only for charitable, religious,

eleemosynary, benevolent, educational or similar purposes, but not held upon a condition requiring return, transfer or conveyance by reason of the dissolution, shall be transferred or conveyed to one or more domestic or foreign corporations, societies or organizations engaged in activities substantially similar to those of the dissolving corporation, pursuant to a plan of distribution adopted as provided in this Act;
d) Other assets, if any, shall be distributed in accordance with the provisions of the articles of incorporation or the bylaws to the extent that the articles of incorporation or bylaws determine the distributive rights of members, or any class or classes of members, or provide for distribution to others;
e) Any remaining assets may be distributed to such persons, societies, organizations or domestic or foreign corporations, whether for profit or not for profit, as may be specified in a plan of distribution adopted as provided in this Act.

These provisions are largely self-explanatory, but two points deserve emphasis:

1. Property held upon express condition requiring that specific action be taken to distribute that property upon dissolution is given a first priority. An illustration of such a condition would be the following provision: "if the college for any reason ceases to be related to the United Methodist Church as determined by the University Senate thereof, this property will be divided in as equal shares as practical among all the United Methodist colleges then operating in the state of Ohio." The lesson here, of course, is that foresight by a donor in establishing such conditions is rewarded under the Model Act. Precision is also rewarded, since subsection (c) indicates that unless the disposition of the property is precisely directed it will be distributed according to a "plan of distribution" adopted by the governing board of the dissolving college.

2. If such conditions are not imposed, the governing board of the failing college will have virtually unfettered discretion

with regard to distribution of those assets, because that board will adopt the "plan of distribution" called for in subsection (c) or design the governing documents of the corporation mentioned in item (d) to accomplish the desired purpose. Again, statutes of individual states vary a great deal, but the Model Act pattern makes clear that neither the religious body nor any other donor will have anything legally to say about assets given by them to the college unless conditions are specified with respect to the gifts. Even if there are adequate legal restrictions in the governing documents of the college to control transfer of the gift property, those are easily changed by the college governing board unless the religious body can control or influence the actions of the board.

Implications of these two points are many. It may be, for example, that the administration and board of directors of the college will wish after dissolution to transfer remaining assets to another individual college or a university system which may be interested in recruiting the students who went there and perhaps, as part of the negotiated package, hiring some key administrators of the failing college. The religious body which directly contributed or was responsible for the contribution of the assets in question may well wish to use those assets such as library collections and remaining endowments for the benefit of other colleges related to the religious body and located nearby or in neighboring states.

Endless possibilities and fact patterns can arise, but the only safe way to secure gifts so that they continue to serve the purposes of the religious body is to specify conditions at the time the gift is given in legally binding documents.

2. Merger and involuntary liquidation

It is possible that the governing board of the financially troubled college would seek to merge with another college without dissolving the corporation of the existing college. It is also possible that creditors or others would seek to dissolve the college involuntarily. It is not within the scope of this paper to discuss all such possibilities, but in most instances conditions which were established for particular assets are likely to be honored first by the courts, if the restrictions were sufficiently precise to be triggered by those eventualities and creditors can be paid.

For example, the Model Act provides in the case of a merger:

> Such surviving or new corporation shall thenceforth be responsible and liable for all the liabilities and obligations of each of the corporations so merged or consolidated. . . .[11]

If the corporation must be liquidated, the Model Act provides in language virtually the same as in voluntary dissolution that after meeting costs of court proceedings and all liabilities and obligations,

> Assets held by the corporation upon condition requiring return, transfer or conveyance, which condition occurs by reason of the dissolution or liquidation, shall be returned, transferred or conveyed in accordance with such requirements.[12]

3. Cy pres

If a state has not enacted a nonprofit corporate statute or the statute does not cover a given factual situation,[13] the common law doctrine of *cy pres* is likely to be applied by courts in most states to direct the disposition of the assets of a dissolved college.[14] In summary this cy pres doctrine is applied to charitable gifts which cannot be given because it has become impossible, impractical, or illegal to do so, and the doctrine provides that courts will seek to redirect the gift assets to similar purposes or agencies.[15]

For example, in accordance with the cy pres doctrine, it was held that the balance of a trust fund created to endow Crawford Institute, an Arkansas institution of higher education controlled by the Methodist Episcopal Church, which ceased operations approximately five years after the death of the donor, should go to a Methodist College more than 125 miles from Crawford Institute. The court decided in favor of the Methodist College in the face of claims by the state of Arkansas and by the local school district, because it seemed apparent that the donor wished his gift to be devoted to a school controlled by the Methodist Conference.[16]

A few observations should be made about the cy pres doctrine:

1. It is an attempt by the courts to adhere to the general intent of the donor. Judges ordinarily will seek to determine that intent from documents or surrounding circumstances which indicate what the donor's wishes were.[17]

2. Most of the corporate nonprofit statutes enacted to specify disposition of assets of a failed nonprofit corporation can be seen as embodying cy pres principles, but there is one substantial difference—under the cy pres doctrine the determination about the disposition of those assets is always made by a court, not the governing board of the dissolving college.[18]

That is a distinction with significant tactical implications for the parties in a dissolution situation. It means, for example, that the board of directors of the college cannot guarantee to any other institution in advance of a judicial determination that the college will transfer the assets in question to that institution. The judge may direct the assets elsewhere. It means also that a sponsoring religious body does not know whether the judge might be willing to direct those assets to a place that the religious body would have them go, for example, to another college related to that religious body rather than to some other charitable institution which may be more attractively situated (in political terms) within the jurisdiction of the court.

It may be possible in some states to have an indication from judicial precedent where such assets will likely be directed. However, cy pres decisions may well be inconsistent or conflicting even within a single jurisdiction,[19] so it may be difficult or impossible to predict with certainty a choice made by the court.

Some states have statutes which govern the disposition of charitable gifts and set out guidance to courts in the use of cy pres doctrine which enhances predictability for the parties.[20] Some states allow the trustees of dissolving corporations to propose a plan of distribution but reserve final approval of that plan to the courts.[21] And other states by common law or statute provide, unlike the Model Act, that at some stage the assets in question simply escheat, i.e., are forfeited, to the state.[22]

Although there is a growing tendency today on the part of courts to restrict the applicability of cy pres to the situation in which a particular charitable purpose has failed or cannot be carried out, there are still many courts which apply the doctrine in areas not meant to be governed by it.[23]

The lesson again: consult local counsel with respect to the law of the states in question and follow that legal advice in planning for contingencies.

B. Disposition of Gift Property in Relationship Severance Situations

Again, the only dominant theme emerging from a review of the law of various states in this area is diversity. Among the legal doctrines which might be applied to such situations are those related to gift and charitable gift subscriptions,[24] trust law and variations thereon,[25] contract,[26] and estoppel.[27] Each variation in the factual situation can bring into play or eliminate the application of these legal doctrines.

It is also fair to say that in this area of property law courts have sometimes indulged in strained logic and melded legal concepts which in textbook theory are quite distinct.[28] For example, judges may reach out to charitable trust doctrine, even though there is not the slightest indication in the facts before the court that the donor ever intended to establish or imply a trust.[29] Further, with these kinds of issues, in contrast to areas of the law such as taxation, securities regulation, or corporations, it is not possible to begin with reference to a statute which is periodically updated by a state legislature. Ordinarily in this area courts look to various strands of common law doctrine which have evolved over the decades, and legal doctrines rise and fall within the legal system. Courts and legislatures are constantly reviewing and changing doctrines like cy pres,[30] so that even within a single jurisdiction the law applicable to charitable institutions is in continuing flux.

Given these kinds of uncertainties within a single jurisdiction, it is even more difficult to identify standards which are common among jurisdictions. There is simply no substitute for careful analysis of the law of the legal jurisdiction involved and possibly the laws of more than one jurisdiction, depending on the location of the parties and property in question.

After considering the tangle of doctrines applied in different circumstances, it seems most useful to avoid a detailed analysis of various legal standards and instead attempt to bring together some general conclusions about how courts view these matters:

1. Intent of the parties

Whether the courts apply trust, gift, contract, or other theories, the initial inquiry is always the same: what did the parties really intend? When the specific fact situation is one for which the parties did not provide, the courts will seek to determine from available documents or surrounding circumstances what the parties expected from their relationship and whether those general expectations furnish guidance about the incident in question.[31]

To illustrate: if a gift were donated to College X with an accompanying letter stating it was "to be used for College X," it makes no difference on the face of the document whether

College X continues to be related, for example, to the Jesuits. All it has to do is continue to be College X. However, if that donor or those claiming on behalf of the donor were able to introduce further correspondence between the college officials and the donor which clearly indicate the reason for the gift was the donor's concern for Jesuit higher education and everyone understood that this gift was given solely because of the relationship of College X to the Jesuits, a court is quite likely to view a departure by College X from a relationship with the Jesuits as forfeiting that gift.

This kind of finding does not always need to be based on formal correspondence; it may be implied from surrounding circumstances. One example might be the disposition of funds which were raised from a religious body or members of a religious body during a capital fund drive in which the college went to great pains to extol the virtues of the relationship to the religious body and the importance of that relationship to the past and future of the college. If, within a year or two after the funds are received, the college moves to dissolve that relationship, a court is likely to search energetically for a theory upon which to return those gifts to the religious body.

It may be, however, that in similar circumstances a court would find for the college if, for example, everyone understood that those funds were to be spent for current operating expenses, rather than preserved in an endowment fund. A move by the college to sever the relationship, even if only a few years later, would likely be viewed by the court as a risk assumed by the donors in making contributions for those purposes without imposing any restrictions upon their use.

In some cases, of course, the donor or representatives of a class of donors may be available to testify about their intentions or their understanding of the donee's representations. Often, however, no such testimony is available. Lacking such direct evidence, courts will resolve disputes over ownership of property by attempting to discern the parties' real intentions. And if these intentions were not set forth in formal documents, they will try to infer them from surrounding circumstances.

2. Identity of the parties

Courts are generally sympathetic about the importance of charitable institutions to the society and their dependence on donations. Judges are not ordinarily anxious to find that gifts made without express conditions should be forfeited by the charitable institution back to the donor.[32] This is particularly the case when the donor is an individual, the gift was made many years before, and the plaintiff now seeking to recover the gift is the donor's distant relative.[33]

3. Disposition of assets

Another question which appears to affect the results of these contests is closely tied to but separate from the identification of the parties: what happens to the assets?[34] Even if the donor has been an individual, the courts may be more sympathetic when a religious body comes in on behalf of the donor and points out that if a college attempting to sever the relationship with the religious body is permitted to take the property in question with it, or if the gift were to revert to the donor's heirs, it will no longer be used for the purposes designated by the donor. If, on the other hand, the court directs the disposition of this property to other colleges still related to the religious body, it will thus be able more closely to approximate the intent of the donor.

Summary Recommendations

1. Overall relationships

These property relationship questions can realistically be analyzed only in conjunction with all other legal as well as informal links between the religious body and college. For analytical purposes this paper has discussed property relationships more or less on their own, but it is likely that in the usual case other links must be considered as well. For example, some representatives of the religious body may sit on the governing board, even if they do not hold controlling votes. So when property questions arise in the midst of some disagreement or crisis in the relationship between college and religious body, there will likely exist means of communication and pressure in addition to any legal documents related to the property being contested. Ordinarily, for example, the property issue is important to a religious body not simply with respect to a single college, but also for its implications for a whole structure of relationships between many colleges and the religious body. The choice of action to be taken is likely to reflect policy issues reaching well beyond a property skirmish at a particular college.

As noted in the Introduction, religious bodies in this nation have recently undertaken a comprehensive review of their involvement in higher education and its institutions. Those considerations have direct implications for an intentional arranging or rearranging of legal relationships between college and religious bodies. Such considerations must include questions about tangible monetary and property contributions from religious bodies to colleges, standards to determine which colleges receive what levels of support, and what protection should be established to insure that those contributions are preserved for the desired purposes.

There are, of course, enormous variations in both absolute and percentage support which religious bodies in this nation contribute to colleges related to them. Many religious bodies contribute substantial direct support; others contribute relatively little direct support.[35] Many religious bodies are responsible for significant indirect economic contributions to related colleges in terms of recruiting students or effectively recommending contributions from other donors; others are not.

In a time of general financial difficulties for many colleges and religious bodies, the careful shaping of these economic relationships deserves some priority in allocating resources and charting the futures of both institutions.

2. Formal and precise restrictions

If either a religious body or a college wishes to establish restrictions, conditions, or qualifications with respect to the use of donated property, it seems far preferable to state these matters in writing than to assume agreement which may or may not exist. No matter what the intentions of the parties or where the equities lie in a particular situation, unless the restrictions are clearly stated, litigation is likely if these relationships deteriorate and the property in question is substantial. Litigation in such situations ordinarily means not only unwelcome legal expenses, but attendant adverse publicity and lingering ill will for all involved.

Any restrictions on donated property must be drafted with precision in order to insure insofar as possible that everyone involved has a clear understanding about these sensitive matters, both to avoid needless disputes and, in the event litigation arises, to limit the discretion of a reviewing judge in disposing of the property.[36] These restrictions may appear in legal instruments, such as gift documents, deeds, and wills, in the governing documents of the college, or even in governing documents of the sponsoring religious body.[37]

Among elements to be considered are a) what events trigger the operation of the restrictions—for example, what happens if the college continues in operation but simply drifts away from the religious body rather than formally renouncing their relationship—b) exactly what happens to the assets in question if the college violates the restrictions—for example, should they revert to the religious body or be distributed to other specified institutions in a particular geographical area— and c) is it appropriate to establish a time limit for such restrictions?

Any restrictions or conditions involved with a particular

gift or pattern of giving should be arranged at the time the gift is made or arranged. These restrictions should be stated in the manner and documents prescribed by local counsel. It may be preferable under certain circumstances for the sponsoring religious body to retain ownership of the property in question and simply permit the college to use it, lease it for a minimal fee or for fair market value, or adopt other strategies as economic needs and other circumstances of the parties dictate.

Even if the giving has already taken place and the relationships are long established, the parties may well be able to agree about appropriate restrictions on the use of property previously contributed, and such agreements should be formalized to bind future representatives of both parties.[38] If the parties perceive that agreement is not likely, they each can separately determine whether to assume the risk in raising questions about past contributions or current patterns of support. It may be argued that if relations between the two institutions have deteriorated to such an extent, either or both may wish to consider whether the relationship should continue at all under such circumstances or whether resources and energies would better be invested elsewhere.

It may be important to establish guidelines not only for gifts of the religious body, but also for gifts made by others, particularly with respect to capital fund drives among constituents of the religious body on behalf of its colleges.

3. Donor initiative

As a general rule, unless the religious body on its own behalf or on behalf of other donors takes the initiative to establish conditions or restrictions on gifts to related colleges, the donor runs a substantial risk of losing any such property in the event the college collapses or moves to dissolve the relationship with the religious body.

There are at least two basic reasons why this is so: as

9 Conclusions and Recommendations

THIS VOLUME has attempted to provide a useful response to a vast range of legal questions which emerge from recent experiences of church related colleges and universities in this nation. We have tried to examine and clarify the legal issues in general terms, taking into consideration the great variety of legal structures and relationships which exist at religiously affiliated colleges.

In reviewing these problems, one is struck by the complexity of the legal problems confronting church related college administrators, the number of these problems which remain to be clarified by courts or legislatures, and the quantity of resources which are required of religiously affiliated colleges to deal adequately with these issues on a continuing basis.

All denominations and religious communities have unique characteristics and glory in their own religious traditions. At the same time many of the legal problems described in this book are shared across denominational lines by most religiously affiliated colleges. Even when these problems emerge from special kinds of denominational structures, it is virtually always informative for representatives of other traditions to examine how the problems were met. The appendices to this study convey both the richness of difference and the sense of commonality which characterize religiously affiliated higher education. As Monsignor Murphy points out in the Preface, this entire study is itself a product of the insights and contributions of many persons from different religious traditions involved in higher education.

New and challenging legal problems will surely continue to arise for religiously affiliated higher education. Those challenges can readily be met, however, if representatives of various traditions are willing to gather together the considerable resources available within each religious community, and to share information, research and analysis which bear upon these problems.

The National Congress on Church-Related Colleges and Universities is an encouraging step toward that kind of combined interdenominational effort. It is hoped that the "unity in diversity" emphasized by Congress organizers will provide new opportunities for dealing with these legal issues as well as the other important matters which appear on the agenda of the National Congress.

State Regulation of Religiously Affiliated Higher Education

As part of an earlier project, the Center for Constitutional Studies conducted an initial review of sixteen states the statutes of which pose serious legal problems for the exercise of religious preference in faculty and staff employment and student admission. Those issues are mostly unrecognized at the moment, but some of them are fundamentally important for religiously affiliated colleges.

We believe there is need for a comprehensive research project to extend and refine that analysis to include all state laws which can impact uniquely upon colleges and universities because of their relationships to religious bodies. A comprehensive treatment should include a state by state analysis which would provide the text of the relevant provisions of the state constitution and statutes, a commentary on the law of that jurisdiction analyzing the constitution, statutes, judicial decisions, and other legal sources, and a short bibliography for each state.

That study would provide a substantial reference resource with respect to the law for each state for anyone involved with church related higher education. It could, in addition, lead to recommendations for changes in model laws like the Model Anti-Discrimination Act and thus could provide the basis for legislative reform across the country.

Unique Constitutional Status of Church Related Colleges and Universities

We also believe it would be useful to explore in depth the special constitutional status of church related colleges. Consideration of that status is important primarily as it defines the constitutionally permissible limits of government regulation of these colleges. Some of those protections are shared with other colleges and universities such as academic freedom and freedom of association. But for certain church related colleges there may, in addition, be special protection which emerges from the Religion Clauses of the First Amendment.

The anticipated benefits to be derived from that analysis of this sort are substantial: a) the project should provide fresh perspectives to basic thinking in this important area of public policy which has yet to be explored in any comprehensive fashion, b) theories developed by the project could be applied in litigation which would seek to establish a constitutional definition of appropriate limits for government regulation of church related higher education, and c) the analysis should also be useful as a resource for testimony before administrative agencies and legislative bodies which are considering a move into new areas or are reviewing existing areas of regulation of religiously affiliated higher education.

Regulation of Religion

Religious organizations are likely to face increasing pressure for government regulation in the future. That pressure is a product in part of the highly questionable activities of some organizations which label themselves "religious." Those activities include the sale of ordinations by mail, high-pressured and misleading fund raising techniques by some media hucksters, recent and dramatic publicity involving various religious cults and the congressional hearings about them, the "brain-washing" charges leveled at certain religious organizations, and misappropriations of charitable donations. These kinds of activities have led to calls for greater financial and other social accountability by religious organizations. Beyond this, however, serious-minded observers are raising basic questions about the privileged status of religious organizations and other charitable institutions in our society, e.g., why should churches and clergy have the benefit of tax-exempt or other tax-favored status?

If this reading is correct, it is likely to have implications for colleges and other institutions related to religious bodies, for fund raising if nothing else. Some representatives of religious organizations have resisted any attempt to define the nature and character of religion for the purposes of government regulation on the grounds that such a process could itself inhibit religious freedoms. In our opinion, however, the pressure for increased government oversight and regulation has advanced to such a stage that religious organizations and their supporters must meet the issue directly and attempt to work out a frame of reference in defining the appropriate relationships between the government and religious organizations. The alternative is that this definitional task is quite likely to be done by government regulators and others with little sympathy for or understanding of religious organizations.

APPENDIX

A The Present State of Roman Catholic Canon Law regarding Colleges and Sponsoring Religious Bodies

Rev. James E. Coriden and
Rev. Frederick R. McManus

A. The State of Canon Law

At this writing, the relevant canon law affecting colleges and universities is in an unusual state of uncertainty and flux. For this reason it is very difficult to give clear and sure answers to the questions raised to church lawyers regarding the property of educational institutions and the relationship of the institutions to their sponsoring religious bodies. There are at least three reasons for the present ambiguous condition of canon law on church property, its acquisition, administration, and disposition (in the 1917 *Code of Canon Law*, canons 1495–1551):

(1) Certain key provisions of the *Code* have not been consistently observed in the United States, e.g., the regulations for the conveyance of church property (cc. 1530–34) including the permission of the "legitimate superior" which is required for a "valid" transaction, and this non-observance has been known and at least tolerated for decades. These failures to comply with the letter of the law were based

Rev. James E. Coriden is Dean of Washington Theological Union. Rev. Frederick R. McManus is Vice Provost and Dean of Graduate Studies at The Catholic University of America. Both are Canon lawyers.

not on disregard or contempt for canonical discipline, but simply on practical necessity and sensible accommodation to the economic realities of the American church. They have been accepted as such even at the highest levels of church authority. However, these non-observances have contributed to a certain lack of clarity and security about the precise demands of church law.

(2) There is virtually no available jurisprudence in this area. Church courts very rarely have disputes involving the ownership and control of property before them. There are almost no formal decisions, and the few there are remain unpublished. The "living law" which arises from the decisions of judges applying and interpreting the law in real cases is simply nonexistent in this part of canon law. The occasional administrative guides which come down from the agencies of the Roman Curia, such as the Congregation for Bishops or the Secretariat of State, have been inadequate to keep the law abreast of the developments in the church in the United States regarding the corporate structure and interaction between sponsoring church bodies and colleges. This entire area of canon law must be judged out-of-date and at least obsolescent.

(3) A new set of canons on church property has been formulated over the past decade, but has not yet been promulgated. The revision of the 1917 *Code of Canon Law* is a process which began (in 1963) even before the end of the Second Vatican Council and has continued to the present time. In 1973 a report was published[1] which recounted the progress made by the subcommission on church property and the general direction of its thinking on the revised canons. A proposed draft of fifty-seven canons for this area of the law was published in 1977[2] by the Commission for the Revision of the Code and sent to all the bishops of the world for their reactions and comment. The bishops' responses were to be returned by the end of October, 1978, but will likely be delayed beyond that time. This proposed law has no legal force as yet, but it gives some sense of the

present thinking of the legislative authority in the church. The draft of proposed legislation in circulation contributes to the unsettled state of the law.

For these and other reasons canon lawyers are unable to provide any summary of clear and practical guidance at this time. A helpful and reliable compendium of answers to the questions being asked by those involved in the schools and churches is simply not possible now. The state of the law does not permit it.

A careful and thorough study of the matter would indeed be welcome. There is genuine need for detailed monographs, with historical background and theoretical foundation, to take their place alongside other valuable but dated studies, e.g., dissertations at the Catholic University of America (*Canon Law Studies*).[3] Such studies, even though their conclusions would be necessarily tentative at the present time, should nonetheless be undertaken.

B. Two Identifiable Trends

The recently circulated draft of canons on church property (referred to above) reveals two distinct directions or trends, mutually interrelated, which can be expected to continue and emerge in any final legislation:

(1) An emphasis on subsidiarity or a heightened sense of local autonomy. The principle of subsidiary function is one of the principles for the direction of the revision of the *Code* which were adopted by the Episcopal Synod of 1967.[4] It is mentioned three times in introductory remarks ("Praenotanda") to the proposed draft of canons on property. Subsidiarity finds expression in several projected canons (e.g., 16, 17, 19, 42, 55–57) which leave to national episcopal conferences or to local bishops matters previously regulated by *Code* legislation or reserved to the authority of the Holy See.

(2) An increased reliance on and conformity with local

civil law. The 1917 *Code* "canonized" civil law in several significant areas, e.g., solemnities of wills, contracts, agreements to resolve controversies, and the proposed, revised canons maintain and extend this tendency, e.g., in labor relations (c. 30), property leases (c. 42), and retirement funds (c. 16). Future church legislation will clearly take greater cognizance of applicable civil law.

These two trends, both authentic and healthy, are easily discernible in the legislation being developed and formulated for the church, and they will surely be embodied in the law when it is promulgated.

C. The Function of American Law

Many of the aims intended by canonical provisions are even more effectively achieved by compliance with the statutes and jurisprudence of American law. In general, the civil law provides secure safeguards and the courts provide fair remedies in such matters as ownership of property and its reservation to a certain use, the dedication of property held in trust for specified purposes, the holding of charitable corporations or trusts to their stated purposes, faithful compliance with terms of bequests, gifts, etc. Values and goals such as these, which have generated many of the canonical regulations surrounding the administration of church property, have been and are being met by the careful observance of American civil law. It is this sense of security and satisfaction in the church with regard to our civil legal system which has occasioned the de-emphasis and partial non-observance of canon law in matters of property. The church senses itself to be in a congenial, serviceable, and reliable legal structure in the United States, and this feeling lessens the need for parallel or additional legal safeguards of its own.

D. McGrath and Maida

Two small treatises have appeared in the past decade on the subject of the ownership and control of church property, and both have achieved considerable notoriety and influence. The first is a study done at the Catholic University of America under a grant from the Raskob Foundation by John J. McGrath, *Catholic Institutions in the United States: Canonical and Civil Law Status.*[5] The more recent was commissioned by the Pennsylvania Catholic Conference and written by Adam J. Maida, *Ownership, Control and Sponsorship of Catholic Institutions: A Practical Guide.*[6]

From the time of their publication canon lawyers have expressed some reservations about the canonical and theological theories, interpretations and positions taken in these two works. It might be useful to mention some of those reservations.

(1) McGrath surely erred in narrowly construing canon 100 of the *Code,* which calls for the constitution of ecclesiastical moral persons by the formal decree of the competent ecclesiastical superior. Since explicit, formal decrees of erection had been issued for virtually no Catholic college, hospital, orphanage, etc., McGrath concluded that they were not moral persons canonically. And, because church property can only be owned by "moral persons constituted as juridical persons by ecclesiastical authority" (cc. 1495 and 1497), he further concluded that the lands, buildings, equipment, etc., belonging to these institutions were not really church property and not subject to canon law. This simplistic canonical reasoning enabled him to reach the further conclusion at civil law that the general public has equitable title to the property of such institutions because they are chartered as charitable corporations under the authority of the state. The civil law of trusts or corporations, however, does not seem to give to the general public any claim to the property of charitable corporations.

McGrath seems also to have taken insufficient account of certain basic norms of the ecclesiastical law, for example, the underlying responsibility of church administrators to employ the formalities of the civil law in order to protect the property they administer (see canon 1523) or the principle that the intentions of the donors must be respected (see canons 1513, 1514, and 1523).

Several years after the publication of the McGrath treatise, in a remarkable letter from the Prefects of the Roman Congregations of Religious and of Catholic Education to the President of the National Conference of Catholic Bishops (November, 1974), the curial officials disowned the "McGrath thesis," stating, "We wish to make clear that this thesis has never been considered valid by our Congregations and has never been accepted."

Although there is a lack of good commentary and authoritative decisions on the point, it is reasonable to construe less formal documents, appointments, letters, negotiations, etc., which recognize and acknowledge the existence of close and dependent relationships between the college, hospital, orphanage, etc., and the sponsoring diocese or religious community, as the acceptable equivalent of a formal decree. Such institutions created, sponsored, funded, administered, and staffed by a church body should certainly be considered ecclesiastical moral persons, and their property has been considered church property in a canonical as well as popular sense. They are subject to canonical legislation, even though that fact may have relatively little practical effect, since they are most often also civilly incorporated and their property subject to many state and federal regulations. As McGrath himself pointed out, the myriad personal influences of trustees, administrators, staff, and employees have a much greater impact on the "Catholic" nature of such institutions than the fact that their property is or is not subject to canon law.

There are indications that the "McGrath theory" was accepted uncritically and put into effect by church-related institutions so as to weaken or dissolve that relationship. On the other hand, the work had the positive effect of bringing to the boards of Roman Catholic institutions a far better representation of the (lay) church community, that is, of the church itself. This was and is in full harmony with sound Catholic ecclesiology and the doctrine of the Second Vatican Council.

(2) Maida begins his treatise by stating that "This work has one overriding purpose: protecting the property rights

of the Church. . . ." That is, indeed, his preoccupation, and it leads him into some recommendations which, like McGrath's, are questionable from both legal and theological points of view. The canonical premises are basically correct; some minor misstatements have been pointed out by reviewers,[7] but they are not of great consequence. The potential for legal jeopardy in the civil sphere resulting from the high levels of control which Maida clearly prefers are spelled out in chapter two of this volume: For example, the concentration of corporate power in a single individual could lead to legal actions not only against the diocese based on a theory of ascending liability, but also against the bishop individually in instances where he failed to exercise requisite diligence in carrying out the responsibilities of a corporate director.

It is Maida's exclusive focus and strong emphasis on control in the hands of the bishop (or the religious superior and council) which tends to distort the notion of the church and its relationship to temporal goods. He recommends (pp. 26, 54) that the bishop be the sole member of the charitable corporations established to own or manage the enterprises carried on in the name of the church, and then he counsels that all of the radical controlling decisions be reserved to the member(s) of the corporation (pp. 60–61). Nowhere in his suggested models of relationships between sponsoring religious bodies and their charitable institutions does he mention the modern organs of collegiality and subsidiarity which he mentions earlier (p. 6), e.g., priests' senates, diocesan pastoral councils, or those more traditional collegial agencies mandated by the *Code,* e.g., diocesan consultors (cc. 423–28), the council of administration (c. 1520), or the administrators of church properties (cc. 1521–23). Neglect of these canonical institutes, which are intended as a restraint upon unitary episcopal power, may render actions of the bishop unlawful or even invalid at ecclesiastical law.

After reading Maida's practical applications one is left with the strong impression that the bishop alone speaks for, decides for, and exclusively represents the local church (and the religious superior and council do the same for a religious community), and that ecclesiastical property is legally safe and surely applied to its proper purposes only when the bishop has total control over it. This is a vision and misconception of the local church, perhaps not intended by the author, in which "church" and "people" are different and distinct (a distinction Maida makes explicitly on the bottom of p. 8), and in which as a practical matter only the bishop can be counted truly trustworthy. It is a most unfortunate vision to begin with when one is trying to build an appropriate legal structure for the ownership and effective use of assets for the church's mission. It is a model of church organization which inadequately embodies the renewed ecclesiology of the Second Vatican Council at the practical level—where it counts.

The following quotations illustrate, with emphasis added, the teaching of the Vatican Council on the collaborative nature of the church and its mission. It should be noted that these solemn documents supersede, in principle and as norms, the existing canon law.

> Everything which has been said . . . concerning the People of God *applies equally to the laity, religious, and clergy.* Pastors . . . know that they themselves were not meant by Christ to shoulder alone the entire saving mission of the Church toward the world. On the contrary, they understand that it is their noble duty so to shepherd the faithful and *recognize their services and charismatic gifts* that all according to their proper roles may cooperate in this common undertaking with one heart.[8]
>
> These faithful are by baptism made one body with Christ and are established among the People of God. They are in their own way made *sharers in the priestly, prophetic and kingly functions* of Christ. They carry out their own part in the mission of the whole Christian people with respect to the Church and the world.[9]
>
> Upon all the laity, therefore, rests the noble duty of working to extend the divine plan of salvation ever increasingly

> to all men of each epoch and in every land. Consequently, *let every opportunity be given them* so that, *according to their abilities and the needs of the times,* they may zealously participate in the saving work of the Church.[10]
>
> Let sacred pastors recognize and *promote the dignity as well as the responsibility of the layman* in the Church. Let them willingly make use of his prudent advice. Let them confidently assign duties to him in the service of the Church, *allowing him freedom and room for action.*[11]
>
> No part of the structure of a living body is merely passive but each has a share in the functions as well as in the life of the body. So too, in the body of Christ, which is the Church . . . the laity . . . *share in the priestly, prophetic and royal office of Christ* and therefore have their own role to play in the mission of the whole People of God in the Church and in the world.[12]
>
> . . . By reason of the gift of the Holy Spirit which is given to priests in sacred ordination, bishops should *regard them* [the laity] *as necessary helpers and counselors in the ministry* and in the task of teaching, sanctifying, and nourishing the People of God.[13]
>
> All priests, both diocesan and religious, participate in and exercise with the bishop the one priesthood of Christ and are thereby meant to be *prudent cooperators of the episcopal order.*[14]

The approach illustrated in the practical applications of Maida's treatise sharply diverges from the attitude assumed in the *Directory on the Pastoral Ministry of Bishops*[15] in conformity with the normative constitutions and decrees of the Second Vatican Council. The first paragraph (n. 133) of the article on "Administration of Church Property" is headed "Participation of the Community in the Administration of Church Property":

> The Bishop takes suitable measures that the faithful may be educated to a sense of participation and cooperation also as regards the temporal goods which the church needs to fulfill her purpose, so that all according to their indi-

> vidual capacities consider themselves co-responsible both in the economic support of the church community and of its works and charities, as well as in the preservation, increase and proper administration of the community's temporalities.

Two further indications that the church officially insists on a sharing of responsibility in the administration of property and the conduct of educational institutions are: (1) the proposed Draft of Canons of *Book Two: The People of God* (cc. 306–8) calls for the appointment of a diocesan finance council and *oeconomus* (business manager) even when the bishop is in full control of his office—an attempt to relieve the diocesan bishop of his taxing overinvolvement in financial administration and to assure careful consultation in matters of money; and (2) the norms for the direction of seminaries[16] recommends that the bishop exercise oversight by means of consultation, respect for the professional competencies of administration and faculty, and a board consisting of those who share concern for priestly formation. Since these forms of collegiality and subsidiarity are required in the educational institution most closely related to the life of the official church, i.e., the diocesan seminary, *a fortiori* the same principles should be applied to Catholic colleges and universities.

To sum up, the "Maida thesis," which has the sound purpose of assuring the protection of church values and interests, represents an extreme more rigid and potentially harmful than the "McGrath theory." Specifically, it seriously neglects the true nature of the church. Aside from the legal implications (above), if ecclesiastical and educational functions are confused, the legitimate academic integrity of educational institutions can be compromised and jeopardized.

E. Assurance of True Faith and Sound Morals

The orthodoxy and orthopraxis of its sponsored institution are a vital and legitimate concern of the church. The faithful and their leaders share responsibility for proclaiming and witnessing to the authentic Catholic tradition both in their personal lives and in their organizational involvements. The positive aspects of this high and serious charge are far more important than the negative. That is, more planning, energy, and resources should go into teaching, publishing, consulting, counseling, and guiding than are expended on investigating, censoring, prohibiting, condemning, and dismissing. And the duty to announce the gospel and promote good moral practice must never be discharged with a historical narrowness or in a spirit of self-righteous repression.

The *Code of Canon Law* lays certain specific responsibilities in this regard upon bishops, religious superiors, pastors, and other officials (e.g., the canon theologian, the censor of books, etc.), but this does not limit the responsibility solely to these officials. Sometimes the means of discharging the duty have been detailed in the legislation, e.g., by visiting schools, censoring books, requiring professions of faith for seminary instructors, etc., but more often they are stated in terms of general surveillance and pastoral concern.

When it comes to translating these responsibilities into the sponsoring relationship between a diocese or religious community and an institution of higher education, it seems a mistake to rely on corporate instruments of total control, such as the one-member corporation where the member has power to remove without cause the Board of Trustees, to appoint and dismiss the chief administrator, to approve the operating budget, etc. This appears misguided for three reasons, one theoretical and two practical:

(1) Such extensive authority concentrated in one person does not accurately represent the nature of the church. The church is a community of faith wherein leadership is shared in a collegial mode. Sole and absolute possession of sweeping powers in the local church is a distortion of the underlying theological reality. The common law of the church already imposes limitations upon the diocesan bishop. Such limitations have already been mentioned in regard to manda-

tory consultation, which, according to the canons, is a significant and necessary part of church administration (c. 105), but they exist also in regard to judicial power, which the bishop is obliged to share with diocesan judges, and may exist even in the case of legislative power: the bishop, although the sole diocesan legislator, is obliged to hold synods at regular intervals (c. 356, § 1); on occasion, he may also recognize a deliberative power in the presbyteral council or senate.

(2) If disputes arise which redound to issues of orthodoxy or orthopraxis, the civil courts will not be of much help. Generally the courts will not attempt to decide such matters; and most would agree that it is better that they do not. In the areas of doctrine and moral practice, legal recourse is of limited value for this reason, and not too much assurance should be drawn from structures of corporate control.

(3) Dangers of prejudice, misjudgment, or arbitrary action are always magnified when great authority is placed in the hands of one person, even though that person be pious and well-intentioned. Likewise, when the controlling group is small and not held to careful consultation, the possibility of peremptory or parochial decisions is increased.

Instead of relying excessively on instruments of corporate control for purposes of maintaining authentic teaching and moral practice, a wide range of measures should be simultaneously and sedulously employed, for example:

–clear declarations of Catholic identity in the purpose clause of the corporate charter and in the by-laws;

–in the case of a membership corporation, the members should consist of a specified group of committed members of the community, e.g., priests' senate, diocesan pastoral council, etc.;

–the trustees or directors should be most carefully chosen persons of high integrity, thoroughly persuaded of the purpose of the institution, a majority of whom should be intelligent, believing, loyal Catholics, both lay and clerical;

—regular and open communications, preferably of a personal and dialogic style, should be maintained between the institution and the sponsoring church body; this should be carried on at various levels, including but not restricted to the episcopal (or provincial) and presidential; a candid annual report should be a part of this exchange;

—the recruitment and appointment of faculty and administrations should be done with great care, with the overall goals of the institution in mind in each instance; Catholic faith, moral probity, and commitment to the aims of the school should be weighted along with the usual academic and professional qualifications.

This web of organizational and personal ties will be a more suitable and effective guarantee of Catholic identity, true doctrine, and good moral witness than an over-reliance on pure corporate control. It will not prevent disputes, disruptions, or deviations from ever occurring, but it will provide a more favorable framework within which to resolve or deal with them charitably, equitably, and peacefully.

F. Canonical Counsel

When specific changes in the relationship between a college and its sponsoring religious body are being contemplated or planned, there is no substitute for personal consultation with a knowledgeable lawyer—a local attorney with experience in the jurisdiction and in the appropriate fields of law—and a canon lawyer with an understanding of present practice and the state of church law. The executive office of the Association of Catholic Colleges and Universities has compiled a list of competent canon lawyers who are available for consultation and will assist its member schools to secure their services.

APPENDIX B Property Relationships: The United Methodist Church and United Methodist Related Colleges

Kent M. Weeks

The history of United Methodist commitment to higher education is remarkable for the great number and variety of institutions launched and for the ecumenical and nonsectarian emphasis not usually associated with church-related colleges. A commission established by the church to review the relationship of the church to higher education concluded, after an exhaustive study, that the church should continue direct relationships with colleges and universities because of (1) the church's theological perspective; (2) Wesleyan tradition and heritage in higher education; (3) concern for a liberally educated laity and clergy; (4) concern for value-centered inquiry; (5) concern for the empowerment of the individual through liberal arts education; and (6) commitment to cultural pluralism and educational diversity.[1]

The church has not taken a possessive view of its institutions, nor has it seen them as an arm of the church to serve only church purposes. The commission found that "The Wesleyan tradition in education has endeavored to avoid narrow sectarianism. Cosmopolitan and ecumenical in nature, Methodist institutions have been open to all." Kingswood

Kent M. Weeks is a practicing attorney in Nashville, Tennessee, and of counsel to the Board of Higher Education and Ministry, The United Methodist Church.

school, founded by John Wesley in England in 1748, took a motto: *In Gloriam Dei Optimi Maximi In Usum Ecclesiae Et Republicae* (To the glory of the most high God in the service of the church and state) that reflected the multiple purposes of Methodism in education. Over 150 years ago, a Methodist bishop reaffirmed this breadth of purpose upon becoming president of DePauw University:

> If by sectarianism is meant that any privilege shall be extended to youth of one denomination above another or that the faculty shall endeavor to proselytize those placed under his instruction or dwell upon minor points controverted between the branches of the great Christian Family, then there is not and we hope there never will be sectarianism here. But if by sectarianism be meant that the professors are religious men and that they have settled views upon Christian character and duty then we ever hope to be sectarian. . . . Our own course is fully determined. Education without morals is pernicious, and to have morals without religious instruction is impossible. Taking then our stand upon the grand and broad platform of evangelical truth, passing by all minor and non-essential points, we shall ever strive to cultivate the moral as well as the mental faculties of those intrusted to our care.

Well over 800 institutions have been related to The United Methodist Church.[2] The history of these institutions is complex due to mergers, closings, and disaffiliations. The majority of the 134 institutions presently related to the church were founded in the period from the Civil War through the turn of the century, although 25 were founded since that time. Sixty-four of the 134 institutions were created through mergers. In addition, 40 institutions formerly related to the church are still operating—14 as state institutions and 26 as independent institutions related to no church or affiliated with another church. A number of distinguished institutions trace their roots to Methodist foundings: Auburn University, Goucher College, Northwestern University, University of Southern California, University of Tennessee-Chattanooga,

Vanderbilt University, Wesleyan University (Connecticut), and Western Maryland College.[3]

Methodist Polity

The United Methodist Church is an international religious denomination and movement that has served this country through its Christian ministry for over 200 years. The structure of the church is neither hierarchical nor congregational, but is connectional. The ecclesiastical term "connectional" denotes a loosely-knit confederation of over 10 million United Methodists and scores of thousands of largely autonomous units, including 43,000 local churches and thousands of church agencies, pursuing their religious mission throughout the world. The fundamental structural unit of the connectional church is the annual conference; there are 114 annual conferences, 73 of which are in the United States, and each one administers UMC ministries within its defined geographical boundaries. Geographical boundaries tend to follow state lines, although in some states there is more than one conference and some conferences cross state lines.

Most UMC colleges maintain their formal and informal relationships with the local annual conferences. Support for the colleges is derived from the conferences. Property relationships are therefore a function of agreements between the college and the sponsoring conference and state law.

Certain educational institutions, primarily those established for blacks following the Civil War, have a relationship with and are funded by national agencies of the UMC, particularly the Board of Higher Education and Ministry (BHEM) located in Nashville, Tennessee. Property relationships are a function of agreements between the college and the sponsoring agency and are subject to the laws of the state in which the college is located.

The local churches and the annual conferences govern their activities in accordance with *The Book of Discipline,* which is revised quadrennially by the General Conference. The General Conference is the overall legislative assembly of the UMC. It convenes every four years and reviews and revises program and policy for the entire "connection." The body of laws adopted by the General Conference is contained in *The Book of Discipline.*

Connectionalism and the Colleges

Since it is the local annual conference to which most UMC colleges are related, it is the annual conferences that have the primary interest in safeguarding UM funds that have been given to colleges. Prior to 1976 the Discipline provided in a general way for the Division of Higher Education and Ministry of the Board of Higher Education and Ministry to take action to protect or recover investments which BHEM or any annual conference had made in capital funds to UM institutions. Disaffiliation from the UMC by several institutions pointed to the need for greater specificity. Accordingly, the 1976 Discipline charges each conference through its board responsible for higher education:

> To guard property and endowments entrusted to the institutions and to maintain and enforce trust and reversionary clauses in accordance with the provisions of the Division of Higher Education under Section 1613.3c.
>
> To confer at once in the event of any institutional change of status with appropriate representatives of the General Board of Higher Education and Ministry. . . . This is only in the event any educational institution, Wesley Foundation, or other campus ministry moves to sever or modify its connection with the Church or violate the rules. . . .

The 1976 Discipline charges the Board of Higher Education and Ministry of the UMC:

> To guard property and endowments entrusted to the institutions and to maintain and enforce adequate trust and reversionary clauses,

and charges the BHEM's Division of Higher Education:

> To preserve and protect resources, property, and investments of The United Methodist Church, or any conference, agency, or institution thereof, in any educational institution, Wesley Foundation, or other campus ministry unit founded, organized, developed, or assisted under the direction or with the cooperation of The United Methodist Church.

The Division is responsible to provide assistance in the case of disaffiliation or discontinuance and to "take such action as is necessary to protect or recover resources, property, and investments of The United Methodist Church, or any conference, agency, or institution thereof, in capital or endowment funds. . . ."

The University Senate, an agency related to the Board of Higher Education and Ministry, is entrusted with the responsibility for approving institutional affiliation with the UMC; the 1976 Discipline provides in part:

> (1) Approval by the senate is prerequisite to institutional claim of affiliation with The United Methodist Church.
>
> (2) Only institutions affiliated with The United Methodist Church through approval by the senate shall be eligible for funding by annual conferences, General Conference, general boards, foundations, or other agencies of The United Methodist Church.

Established originally to assure the quality of institutions that sought to claim UMC affiliation, the University Senate has functioned in recent years as an advisory body to institutions and to church agencies on important institutional problems. It has approved requests from institutions seeking disaffiliation from the UMC.

This paper deals primarily with the question of what happens to church funds in the event of a college's disaffiliation from the UMC. Disaffiliation should be distinguished from the issue of dissolution, which is not addressed in this paper. In the event of dissolution or bankruptcy, the question of distribution of assets, although complex, can be understood with reference to the Model Non-Profit Corporation Act.[4]

In the case of disaffiliation, however, the guidelines are unclear. The variables to be considered include the intent of the parties, the nature of the funds—whether capital, endowment, or operating funds—and the provision, if any, for disposition of the funds. The issue of property relationships is important, not only with respect to a particular college, but also for implications for relationships between the UMC and its other colleges.[5] Three case studies, each of which occurred before the 1976 Discipline was written, illustrate the complexity of issues that may arise in the event of disaffiliation.

Case I: Disaffiliation and Transfer to State System

The college had been affiliated with the UMC since 1843 and the property was owned by the annual conference for that geographical area. Throughout its history, the college's financial base had been marginal, although in the 1950s and early 1960s the college enjoyed an enrollment boom and saw an influx of students from the east coast. When enrollment declined in the late 1960s, the college became more dependent on students from the surrounding area and there was a decline in dormitory occupancy. Newly established community colleges competed for nearby students.[6]

By 1974, serious financial problems had developed and the administration perceived that its options for maintaining a viable institution were limited. The college initiated negotiations with the governor and the state Board of Higher Education with the objective of revitalizing the college as a state institution. Following political and legislative negotiations, the state agreed to take over the college on the condition that the college repay its substantial accumulated deficit. Although the college lacked endowment, it did own property adjacent to the campus that could be sold to raise funds to pay off the deficit. The sponsoring conference approved unanimously in 1974 the transfer of the college to the state, provided the state agreed to continue to operate the college as an institution of higher education.

In correspondence with the college, the Board of Higher Education and Ministry took the position that the procedure for disaffiliation should include consultation with BHEM and approval by its University Senate. If there were endowment funds or property that belonged to the church, they should be transferred to the appropriate church agencies. In this case no such assets were identified. The University Senate reviewed the entire process and approved disaffiliation in 1976.

A fundamental point is that the sponsoring conference agreed to the transfer and believed that the church had no residual interests in the assets of the college. The determination of whether the church does in fact have residual assets is not easily accomplished, because records are not always clear on this point. The college is now operating as a state institution.

Case II: De Facto Disaffiliation

A large university, affiliated with the UMC from its founding, had long assumed that it was an independent nonsectarian institution. On the other hand, never having been formally notified, the BHEM assumed that the university was still related to the UMC. A routine letter sent to the university by BHEM requesting basic data brought the question to the fore in 1973. In the context of the climate of church-state litigation, the university challenged the claim that it was church related. Claiming that it had not been affiliated with the UMC since 1948, it requested that BHEM conform its records to the university's long-standing nonsectarian and nonaffiliated status.

This case raised for the first time the question of who determines for the university and for the church whether an institution is related to the UMC. BHEM's University Senate reviewed the request for disaffiliation—although the very process was regarded by the university as an unwarranted violation of its independent status—and approved the request. The University Senate determined that there were no restricted assets held by the university for the UMC or other church agencies and that the university had obtained an independent status even though certain members of its board were selected by the annual conference.

If the relationship between an institution and the church slowly erodes over a period of years and the institution at some point in time claims an independent status, what, if anything, can the sponsoring church do? Unless there are assets specifically restricted for use by the church—and in most cases such determination is difficult to make and requires the full cooperation of the institution in opening its records—the church must accept a *fait accompli.* The university argued in this instance that *de facto* disaffiliation had occurred many years ago; the university sought recognition from the BHEM University Senate of *de jure* disaffiliation.

Case III: Disaffiliation and Church-State Litigation

In a widely publicized case, a college disaffiliated from the UMC after having been a party in church-state litigation. Twice within a ten-year period a state program of aid to institutions of higher education had been challenged and twice the college had been named as a defendant. In 1975 the college decided to "terminate completely the church affiliation to achieve an unequivocal legal position as an independent liberal arts college"; the effect of this action was to make the college eligible for state funds.

The college had been affiliated with the UMC since its founding and had taken pride in its affiliation. In 1964 a major fund-raising campaign was undertaken by the sponsoring conference to raise money for various institutions related to the conference, including the college. This campaign raised for the college about $400,000 to permit the college to expand its facilities. The pamphlet used to promote the campaign said that the college's share of the funds "will go toward an expansion program which will provide an opportunity for 300 additional students to benefit from higher education in a Methodist-related college that recognizes Christian values as fundamental to all truth." In its promotional literature the college described itself as a "liberal arts college related to the Methodist Church." In the early 1970s, a time when many colleges re-examined relationships with sponsoring churches, the college articulated its relationship in this way:

> It is independent in the sense that it is owned and governed by an autonomous, self-perpetuating board of trustees. It is historically affiliated with the United Methodist Church through its founding, the voluntary participation of the church in its life and work, and an effort on the part of the college itself to reflect this fraternal relationship, in a manner consistent with its character as a free academic and corporate community, in at least some of the services it performs and in the spirit of its work.

The college had received operating funds from its sponsoring conference, but in 1974 the college advised the conference that it did not wish to be included in future budgets. The following year, the college terminated its affiliation with the UMC. The college wanted to remain a viable liberal arts institution: the annual report for 1975 indicated that as an independent institution, it would receive $373,000 from the state—far more than it had received from its sponsoring conference in *recent* years.

The BHEM University Senate, after a review by a committee, accepted the college's decision to terminate its relationship. The Senate requested that, pursuant to the Discipline, the church undertake proceedings to recover church assets. Specifically contemplated was recovery of the capital funds raised for the college during the 1964 conference campaign and other assets, if they could be identified, provided by the conference in earlier periods. Substantial debate occurred within the BHEM regarding its obligation to seek a recovery of assets. The college assured BHEM that neither college endowment nor any other assets included restrictions that the assets be used for church purposes. Ultimately, no action was taken to seek recovery of funds from the 1964 conference campaign or from prior campaigns.

Conclusion

What conclusions can be drawn from the case studies and from the church's understanding of its responsibility with respect to church funds given to colleges who seek disaffiliation from the UMC? Clearly the UMC through its agencies and through annual conferences has a fiduciary responsibility to recover assets that have been designated for the use of the church. In carrying out that responsibility, however, there are several problems: the identification of the assets that are restricted to church use, the political problem of whether or not the church should risk a confrontation with the college in going after the assets, and the problem of where to distribute the assets once secured. The church is primarily concerned about the recovery of endowment funds, although in some instances it may wish to seek recovery of capital raised in conference campaigns.

If the assets have been restricted by donors to use for church purposes, and if there is documentation to this effect, then the issue is straightforward, and the church should, according to the Discipline, seek to recover such assets. The church may not always have access to such records; the records themselves may be inadequate or imprecise; and the church may have to rely upon the good faith of the college in this regard.

In a 1947 case, an annual conference requested an opinion of the Judicial Council—which functions as a supreme court for the UMC in that it issues opinions interpreting the Discipline that are binding upon the church. The conference was preparing to transfer the property of Lander College to the community of Greenwood, South Carolina. The Judicial Council ruled that, pursuant to the 1944 Discipline, the conference could transfer the property. However, should any trust funds have been "donated on condition that said College remain the property of and under the control of the South Carolina Conference," the distribution of such assets was a matter of property rights controlled strictly by civil law and probably not subject to the jurisdiction of the Judicial Council.

It is essential, therefore, for the church to be fully informed about the existence of any restricted assets held by the college and to negotiate early for a return of the assets. The church should have ample notice of disaffiliation and access to an audit and other documents to make a determination of whether assets are so restricted. Thus far, the discussion has centered on recovery of restricted assets. In addition, the church may seek to recover assets raised in a conference campaign and designated for a UM college. Funds provided for current operations of an institution are probably not recoverable should an institution disaffiliate.

How does the church decide whether or not to seek recovery of assets that the college is not willing to yield? If an institution has moved away from the church over a long period of time—as in Case Study II—and in the absence of specific restrictions on assets, the church is not in a good position to seek recovery. Even in Cases I and III, in which the church-college relationship was clear, it was difficult for the BHEM to attempt to identify and recover assets without the support of the sponsoring conference. A conference may be reluctant to take action because the resulting publicity would be harmful to both the conference and the college. In a connectional church there must be close coordination between the conference and the church agency entrusted with the responsibility for higher education, the Board of Higher Education and Ministry. If the conference and the presiding bishop do not want to take action, as a practical matter it is difficult for BHEM to initiate action.

If restricted assets, endowment funds, or capital funds are recovered, how should the funds be distributed? Ultimately state law will govern the disposition of assets. There are few precedents to guide the church in the effort to recover and distribute assets. One can assume, however, that in the case of an institution related to a conference, if there are other higher education institutions in the conference or Wesley Foundations, the funds would be kept within the conference and used for higher education purposes.

Despite all of the hurdles described thus far, BHEM must make clear the fact that the church has the obligation, indeed the fiduciary responsibility, to seek recovery of *restricted* assets. Such a position is defensible in a court of law. Beyond the legal issue, there is an ethical issue of assuring that funds designated for United Methodist higher education continue to be used to carry on that mission.

APPENDIX C

Property Relationships of Southern Baptist Colleges

Preston H. Callison

Almost without exception, Southern Baptist institutions of higher education are owned and operated by eleemosynary corporations chartered by the states in which the colleges or seminaries are located. They have all the rights, powers, and limitations provided by the laws of the various states. Yet the institutions have equitable and legal ties to the sponsoring churches, state conventions, and the Southern Baptist Convention to the extent that they are popularly considered to be "owned by," "sponsored by," or "affiliated with" the various Baptist entities.

Charter Limitations

Legally, the only tie is usually by limitation on the powers of the corporation by specific provisions of the charters. Most charters provide that they cannot be amended without the specific action of the sponsor (which may be a church, local association of churches, state convention, or the Southern

Preston H. Callison is senior partner of the law firm of Callison, Tighe, Nauful, and Rush in Columbia, South Carolina, and of general counsel to the South Carolina Baptist Convention as well as a member of its Executive Committee.

Baptist Convention). Most governing boards are elected by the sponsoring body, and the trustees are usually required to be members of churches of the sponsoring body, e.g., each trustee of Furman University is elected by the South Carolina Baptist Convention and must be a member of a cooperating local South Carolina Baptist church. The charter cannot be amended without the approval of the convention.

This pattern varies from state to state and from institution to institution. Colleges tend to move naturally toward a more independent status as their income from non-Baptist sources grows in proportion to the funds from Baptist sources. The first step toward independence is often a move to permit non-Baptist and out-of-state persons to serve on the board. The next step is to ask that the board or a portion of the board be made self-perpetrating so that the influence of the sponsor is diminished and the other contributor groups may be represented. Seldom is this trend reversed, although these proposed changes often cause deep conflict in sponsoring conventions which must approve the charter changes and often result in a diminished sense of responsibility for sponsor support and ultimately may lead to complete independence.

Deed Reservations

A diminishing number of colleges are in whole or in part operated on lands which have a deed reservation which will cause a reversion to the private donor of the land or to the sponsoring convention in the event of attempt to sell the real estate or upon dissolution of the corporation. These reverters are often effective in discouraging a sale of the assets of an institution, but such reservations have become rarer as institutions have expanded or relocated onto acquired properties which have no reversion. Sound planning usually shows that it is poor economy to depend on donated lands with reservations and encourages the purchase of suitable sites which are not encumbered by the reservations.

Usually, the conventions have released or subordinated these reverters in order to permit the college to mortgage its real estate to finance capital improvements.

Trust Relationships

The courts of equity do acknowledge a trust relationship between the college and its trustees and the donor or sponsor if trust conditions are contained in the documents of the college and sponsoring convention, but the courts are reluctant to interfere with the operation of a college in the absence of a clearly stated trust relationship. This tie is particularly weak in respect to Southern Baptist institutions for a number of reasons.

First, there is no single Southern Baptist hierarchy in the state or nation. Most contributions to the institution from church sources come from specially designated gifts from the church members made directly to the college or from a share of the unrestricted gifts of church members to the churches. Baptist churches are autonomous congregational entities, sometimes incorporated but most often unincorporated. The relationship of the churches to the conventions and to the colleges is purely voluntary. The convention cannot assess the churches nor can the convention interfere with the churches' autonomy. The church-convention relationship is characterized as one of cooperation rather than authority.

Since the colleges derive the majority of their resources from nonchurch sources, the courts have held that the churches have no greater claim on the assets of the college than outside contributors have. In the case of *Trustees of Baptist Female College of Liberty Association, et al.*, v. *Barron County Board of Education*, Ky. 192, 228 S.W. 19, the Court held:

> There is no ground whatever for holding that the proceeds of the sale, after discharging the schools indebtedness, belong to the Liberty Association or any of the

> churches comprising the Association. While it is true that the school was a Baptist Institution and was supported principally by Baptists, and the Liberty Baptist Association had the power to elect Trustees, there is nothing in the act, or conditions accompanying the donations, which the Trustees were authorized to receive to indicate that they were for the benefit of Liberty Association or any of the churches.

The Court referred to the provisions of the charter which provided that donations were to be held by them "for the use and benefit of said institution, and according to the intention of the donor, or donors . . . and not otherwise."

This Kentucky case is one of the few reported cases concerning the final distribution of assets of a Baptist school and lays down the principle that unrestricted gifts to colleges are not to be construed as gifts to the sponsoring churches and will not be allowed to be distributed to the sponsoring church in the absence of a clear intent in the act or trust instruments.

The Nebraska case of *Hobbs, et al.,* v. *Board of Education of Northern Baptist Convention* (1934), 253 N.W. 629, holds:

> Donations to a college without other condition than that they be used for the purpose of erecting buildings and maintaining a college for education of the young do not constitute a trust, but are at most gifts upon condition . . . whether or not a trust is created depends upon the language of the instrument under which the donation is made, the intention of the donor gleaned from the words used, and the purpose sought to be accomplished.

The law jealously protects a trust but it also resolves doubts in favor of a minimum of restrictions on the use of property in the hands of the donee. A gift given by a church to a college is not subject to trust restrictions unless the trust is specifically defined in the documents. The churches would be reluctant to challenge this proposition of equity, since the churches themselves receive unrestricted donations which cannot be returned to the donor when church policies or practices change so as to make the donor unhappy. Similarly, gifts from churches to the colleges, either directly or through the conventions, do not of themselves create a trust which will be enforced by the courts.

Yet, built into the system of Southern Baptists are many documents which form the basis of moral trust obligations, which may or may not be enforcible in the courts of equity. These are identified as follows:

(1) Institutions have provisions in charters, constitutions, bylaws, actions of the trustees, and operational directives which may identify an obligation to the donors as to the use of assets. A donation may be made to a particular program upon the presentation to the donor of brochures, resolutions, plans and objectives identifying and promoting specific needs to which the donor may be interested in donating. This may result in a donation which is subject to a condition, e.g., to be used in the construction of a science building, which leaves no trust implications after the use of the funds. It may result in a restricted gift or endowment in which the fund is to be used to operate a specified building or program, which may result in a trust relationship. On the other hand, the gift, in most instances, will have no trust implications and may be used as the college sees fit.

(2) The sponsoring conventions have charters, bylaws, statements of business and financial policy, resolutions, committee reports, and many other written evidences of conditions which might limit the use of funds by an institution.

We find no reported cases which treat the trust implications of the Southern Baptist system of institutional support. While it is safe to assume that the college can carry on its ordinary functions and may contract with third parties without fear that the sponsor will interfere with its power to contract in the ordinary course of business, in the event of an extraordinary disposition of corporate assets or upon dissolution, a good case can be made for a trust relationship as to the equity of the institution. Some of the arguments for this trust relationship are listed as follows:

State and Southern Baptist Convention charter declarations, bylaws, program statements, and statements of business and financial policy usually identify an intent to support, foster, and monitor Christian colleges, which, in themselves, would not be the basis for a trust limitation. Convention resolutions and other actions seek to impose further limitations upon the institutions. Unilaterally, these documents probably would not create any trust relationship, but when weighed in the light of ongoing participation by the institution in the formulation of the limitations and the responses of the institution to them, historically, a trust may have been created. College presidents and other representatives attend and participate in the meetings of the state and Southern Baptist conventions, executive boards, and committees, and report regularly to the conventions, in respect to their budgets, plans, and programs. They are sensitive to the requests and mandates of the sponsoring conventions and cultivate a close relationship with the convention. The institutions usually acquiesce in the actions of the convention on a moral premise, although they seldom acknowledge convention action as a legal mandate. Cooperation with the convention encourages a larger flow of funds and assures the benefits of the promotional and public relations support of the conventions.

On the other hand, the college cannot acknowledge the authority of the convention to determine policy or interfere with academic decisions which could cause a loss of accreditation. Accreditation agencies accept the proposition that the sponsor may determine the purpose of the institution, but it may not interfere with the institution's operation within that purpose. This dual relationship has caused most conventions to loosen the ties and to resort to more subtle influences to attain their objectives through the college.

It might be said that the lack of certainty in respect to

the property relationships between the college and the convention is a mystery which makes the system work. More precision in legal definition of relationships could cause a breakdown in the Southern Baptist system. The assumptions of the donors and of the donees tend to accommodate the purpose of each although they may not coincide and may, in fact, conflict if fully documented. One managment consultant has concluded that the Southern Baptist system theoretically cannot work; but it does in fact work at least as effectively as does the system of denominations having more centralized control.

Southern Baptist Convention

The institutions related to the Southern Baptist Convention are more closely tied to the convention than are typical institutions affiliated with state conventions. Southern Baptists are said to own and operate six seminaries and support a seventh Bible institution, known as the American Baptist Seminary, which is also supported by the National Baptist Convention. There is little question but that the seminaries, by their charters, bylaws, and trustee actions, and by the charters, bylaws, statements of business and financial policy, program statements and resolutions and other actions of the Southern Baptist Convention and its incorporated executive committee, are not independent of the convention. Most of their operating revenues and capital assets are provided by the cooperative program funds of the Southern Baptist Convention, which are derived from the churches, through the state convention, and the Southern Baptist Convention Treasury.

All trustees are elected by the convention. Charters conform to the convention directives and may not be amended without the consent of the convention. Their purpose is primarily to teach and train persons for the ministry and in the knowledge and skills required by the churches, institutions, boards, and commissions of the convention in carrying out the convention's programs. Public funds are not used by the seminaries and a very nominal fee is charged to the student in lieu of tuition. The convention pays almost the entire cost of development and operation of the seminaries. Semi-annual budget reports to the convention or its executive committee are required by the seminaries and the seminaries participate regularly in the preparation processes of the Southern Baptist budgets. Some non-Baptist gifts are received by the institutions but there is no question but that the contributors are fully aware of the limited purpose of the seminaries and of the close ties which the seminaries have to the convention. A gift to a seminary is clearly a gift to the propagation of the gospel by Southern Baptist churches.

The seminaries do not alter their program structures without conforming to the program statements of the convention. Proposed changes in program statements are circulated to all Southern Baptist institutions for study before adoption. If the operation of a seminary is in conflict with the program statement, the convention is requested to change the convention's program statement to conform. If the request is refused, the seminary is expected to conform to the convention's wishes.

Capital expenditures are budgeted by the convention and require convention approval. Property acquisitions require convention approval, and approval of the convention is required for the mortgaging or disposition of any real property. The seminaries are given the power to transact business in the normal course of operations, but ultimate disposition of the assets would undoubtedly be limited in the unlikely event that the courts are called upon to settle a property dispute.

Matters of General Trust Law

The use of the word "trustees" to designate the managing board of a college has a historic meaning, and emphasis is placed upon the trust relationship to the constituency, beneficiaries, and sponsors in addition to the ordinary managerial and policy duties of the trustee to the corporation. In a sense, the corporation is the trustee of the charity, and the trustees, acting for the corporation, have a fiduciary obligation to preserve the assets of the college, to be loyal to the college in situations of conflicts with other interests, and to carry out the purpose of the institution. *Stern* v. *Lucy Wells Hayes National Training School*, 368 F. Supp. 536 (DDC 1973) and 381 F. Supp. 1003 (DDC 1974). *Gilbert* v. *McLeod Infirmary* (S.C.) 64 SE 2d 424.

The trust responsibilities of the Board of Trustees are set out in the case of *Lynch* v. *John M. Redfield Foundation*, 9 Cal. App. 3d 293, 88 Cal. Reptr. 86, 81 ALR 3d 1284, as follows:

> Assets of a charitable corporation are impressed with a Trust. . . . Members of the board of directors of such a corporation are essentially trustees. . . . In making investments of trust funds the trustee of a charitable trust is under a duty similar to that of the trustee of a private trust. From the standpoint of sound legal practice the only technique to be employed by the directors of a charitable corporation in California in the performance of their duties is that of compliance with *strict trust principles*. It should be noted that, while directors of charitable corporations are exempt from personal liability from the debts, liabilities or obligations of the corporation, they are not immune from personal liability for their own fraud, bad faith, negligent acts, or other breaches of duty.

Contractual Relationship

While the trust relationship may be too indefinite for judicial enforcement, in the absence of third parties it is safe to assume that there exists a contractual relationship between the sponsoring convention and the institution which could be enforced in the courts. The institutions share in the convention funds, participate in the budget processes, acquiesce in the convention actions, and generally accept the relationship as set out in the convention charter, constitutions, bylaws, business and financial policies, and program statements.

Conclusion

Due to the absence of a central authority in Southern Baptist and State Baptist conventions, the interrelationships of the many separate entities make it impossible to generalize as to property rights of convention-related colleges. The colleges derive their legal power from state corporate charters and are limited by state corporate laws. They are all free to conduct ordinary business relationships and academic processes without the intervention of the conventions, but they are not ethically or legally free to dispose of assets or operate institutions in conflict with their purposes as stated in the charters and documents creating them. Contributions from conventions do not inhibit the colleges' power to act independently in contracting with third parties and in meeting accreditation requirements in respect to academic and administrative freedom, but convention actions, constitutions, bylaws, program statements, statements of business and financial policy, resolutions, and other actions, along with the institution's own corporate documents, may form the basis of a trust relationship to the convention which affects the use and disposition of the properties.

The independent autonomous status of the churches, the state conventions, the Southern Baptist Convention, and of the colleges and seminaries of each convention cause these relationships to be varied and vaguely defined. It is easily possible that the uncertainties as to the relationships are mutually advantageous to the institutions, the conventions, the churches, and the membership, since Southern Baptist church membership includes a broad spectrum of theological and philosophical perspectives. The emphases and purposes of the institutions vary greatly, but the churches voluntarily contribute to the support of all the institutions through the cooperative program of giving to state and Southern Baptist causes. The voluntary aspect of the system restricts the institution to programs which are acceptable to the churches. Legal conflicts are rare, since such adversary confrontations in secular courts are considered to be in conflict with Paul's admonition to settle disputes within the church. Institutions sometimes grow away from the churches by mutual consent, but the flow of substantial support from the churches exerts an influence upon the colleges which may be more effective than definite legal ties would be. Traditional ties are strong among Baptist institutions, and among the strongest traditions are those which require that the churches, the state conventions, the Southern Baptist Convention, and the institutions of each remain autonomous but tied together by common purposes rather than by well-defined legal relationships. The result has been that Southern Baptists have grown in numbers and wealth in an era when many major church groups are dwindling.

Notes

Introduction

1. Robert P. Parsonage, *Church-Related Higher Education* (Valley Forge: Judson Press, 1978), a study sponsored by the National Council of Churches; *A College-Related Church, To Give the Key of Knowledge, Endangered Service,* and *Toward 2000* (all Nashville: National Commission on United Methodist Higher Education, 1976); Edgar M. Carlson, *The Future of Church-Related Higher Education* (Minneapolis: Augsburg Publishing House, 1977); Earl J. McGrath, *Study of Southern Baptist Colleges and Universities, 1976–1977* (Nashville: Education Commission of the Southern Baptist Convention, 1977); John J. McGrath, *Catholic Institutions in the United States: Canonical and Civil Law Status* (Washington, D.C.: The Catholic University of America, 1968); Adam J. Maida, *Ownership, Control and Sponsorship of Catholic Institutions: A Practical Guide* (Harrisburg, Pa.: Pennsylvania Catholic Conference, 1975); "Canonical and Legal Fallacies of the McGrath Thesis on Reorganization of Church Entities," *Catholic Lawyer* 19 (1973), 275–86; Garry A. Greinke, *Survival with a Purpose: A Master Plan Revisited* (Washington, D.C.: Lutheran Education Conference of North America, 1978). In addition, a subcommittee of the Association of Catholic Colleges and Universities is currently engaged in drafting a statement on the mission and purpose of Roman Catholic colleges.

2. "The U.S., as befits a society of laws, has always been a litigious land. But the past quarter-century has brought a particularly explosive burst of growth in the legal industry. . . . These developments have brought about a virtual revolution in American society: an all-pervasive invasion by courts, laws and administrative agencies into areas that had previously been ruled by custom, practice or plain old-fashioned private accommodation. . . . Chief Justice Burger: 'We may well be on our way to a society overrun by hordes of lawyers, hungry as locusts, and brigades of judges in numbers never

before contemplated'" (*Time*, April 10, 1978, p. 56). And see "The Chilling Impact of Litigation," *Business Week*, June 6, 1977, pp. 58–64. See also "Let's Make the Law an Access to Justice," 64 *ABA Journal* 639 (1978), an editorial by William B. Spann, Jr., then president of the American Bar Association.

3. From the viewpoint of religiously affiliated colleges, the exercise of governmental power with the greatest potential for interference with a college's religious character and identity would undoubtedly be restrictions placed on the exercise of religious preference in the employment of faculty and staff and in the recruitment and admissions of students. This issue is discussed in chapters four and five. For samples of strong criticism of the "stifling bureaucratic requirements" accompanying federal aid to higher education see the remarks of Derek Bok, President of Harvard, reported in *Harvard University Gazette*, June 13, 1975, p. 1, col. 2; *Chronicle of Higher Education*, June 23, 1975, p. 1, cols. 2–4; *N. Y. Times*, June 25, 1975, p. 48, cols. 6–8; and see the comments of Kingman Brewster, then President of Yale, reported in *Yale Alumni Magazine*, April 1975, pp. 34–35. For more analytical treatment of the problem of governmental regulation in higher education, see Robert M. O'Neil, "God and Government at Yale: The Limits of Federal Regulation of Higher Education," 44 *U. Cincinnati L. Rev.* 525 (1975); and Dallin H. Oaks, "A Private University Looks at Government Regulation," 4 *Journal of College and University Law* 1 (1976). Two recent studies have assessed the costs of governmental regulations to institutions of higher education. Carol Van Alystne and Sharon L. Coldren, *The Costs of Implementing Federally Mandated Social Programs at Colleges and Universities* (Washington, D.C.: American Council on Education, 1976); and Robert A. Scott. "More Than Greenbacks and Red Tape: The Hidden Costs of Government Regulations," *Change* 10 (April 1978), 16–23.

4. Edith L. Fisch, *Charities and Charitable Foundations* (Pamona, N.Y.: Land Publications, 1974), pp. 471–500; John Horty, *Hospital Law* (1978), p. 1; William E. Knepper, *Liability of Corporate Officers & Directors* (Indianapolis: Allen Smith Company, 1973), §1.14 Nonprofit Corporations; Kristen M. Brown, "The Not-For-Profit Corporation Director: Legal Liabilities and Protection," *Federation Insurance Counselor Quarterly*, Fall 1977, pp. 57–87.

5. These issues are sufficiently similar that it would likely be mutually beneficial for representatives of these nonprofit institutions to share in analysis and planning to meet common problems, particularly in the areas of property relationships and exposure to liability.

6. See Manning M. Pattillo, Jr., and Donald M. MacKenzie, *Church-Sponsored Higher Education in the United States* (Washington, D.C.: American Council on Education, 1966), especially pp. 30–53; see also, Parsonage, note 1 supra.

7. Ibid.

1. Legal and Structural Relationships

1. It should be emphasized that this study does not deal with the underlying policy questions of whether or how much influence by a religious body upon colleges is desirable. There is likely to be a wide divergence of opinion about those foundational questions, but they are outside the scope of this study. It may be, however, that this discussion of legal issues will inform that policy debate.

2. The Austin College–Synod of Red River Presbyterian Church, U.S. covenant, provides a helpful example of the kind of process which may be involved when college and sponsoring religious body leaders work together in negotiating and setting forth formally the terms of their relationship. Information about that process and the covenant may be obtained from John D. Mosely, Director, Center for Program and Institutional Renewal, Austin College, Sherman, Texas 75090.

3. These structural elements are commonly used to define "control" both in management analysis, e.g., the definitions and illustrations with respect to hospital governance set forth in the American Institute of Certified Public Accountants Exposure Draft, Ernst and Ernst pamphlet No. 38791 "Financial Reporting Developments," June 1, 1978 at p. 13, and in the formal provisions of statute and regulation, e.g., I.R. Reg. 1.6033–2 (g) (5).

4. See, e.g., Ohio Rev. Code Ann. §1702.29 (B), Ind. Code §23-7-1.1–11.

5. See, e.g., Harris v. Board of Directors of Community Hospital of Evanston, 55 Ill. App. 3d 392, 370 N.E. 2d 1121 (1977).

2. Liability Issues

1. Ray J. Aiken, John F. Adams, and John W. Hall, *Liability: Legal Liabilities in Higher Education: Their Scope and Management* (Washington, D.C.: Association of American Colleges, 1976), a reprint of two articles which originally appeared in 3 *Journal of College and University Law* 3, 215 (1976).

2. See Introduction, note 2, supra.

3. Howard L. Olek, *Non-Profit Corporations, Organizations and Associations* (Englewood Cliffs, N.J.: Prentice-Hall, 1974), pp. 225–29; "Liability for Torts of Volunteers," 82 *ALR* 3d 1213, 1215 (1978); 15 Am. Jr. 2d *Charities* §190 (1976).

4. Robert M. Hendrickson, "'State Action' and Private Higher Education," 2 *Journal of Law and Education* 53 (1973); see, e.g., Spark v. Catholic University of America, 510 F. 2d 1277 (D.C. Cir. 1975); Coleman v. Wagner College, 429 F. 2d 1120 (2d Cir. 1970); Belk v. Chancellor of Washington Univ., 336 F. Supp. 45 (E.D. Mo. 1970).

5. See Note, "Common Law Rights for Private University Students:

Beyond State Action Principles," 84 *Yale Law Journal* 120 (1974), in which the authors argue that in order to provide fundamental fairness the common law rights and protections of private associations should be applied to students at private universities. See also John A. Beach, "Fundamental Fairness in Search of a Legal Rationale in Private College Student Discipline and Expulsions," 2 *Journal of College and University Law* 65 (1974), in which an experienced private university attorney argues that public policy and contract law are wholly adequate and appropriate to provide judges with sufficient grounding to ensure fundamental fairness for students of private colleges.

6. Ray J. Aiken, "Tort Liability of Governing Boards, Administrators and Faculty in Higher Education," 2 *Journal of College and University Law* 129 (1975); William C. Porth, "Personal Liability of Trustees of Educational Institutions," 2 *Journal of College and University Law* 143 (1975).

7. John C. Tucker, "Financial Exigency-Rights, Responsibilities, and Recent Decisions," 2 *Journal of College and University Law* 103 (1975).

8. Lee v. Lon Morris College, No. 1038629, District Ct. of Harris Co., Texas, 189th Judicial District (1975).

9. Oliver, Trustee v. The Catholic Society of Religious and Literary Education, et al., Civil Action No. 73–H–1229 U.S. District Ct. for the Southern District of Texas, Houston Division.

10. Barr v. The United Methodist Church, et al., No. 404611 San Diego Superior County Court (1977).

11. *Newscope*, Jan. 5, 1979, p. 2.

12. See, e.g., Malloy v. Fong, 37 Cal. 2d 356, 232 P. 2d 241 (1951); Miller v. International Church of the Four-Square Gospel, Inc. 225 Cal. App. 2d 243, 37 Cal. Rptr. 309 (1964); Roman Catholic Archbishop v. Superior Court, 15 Cal. App. 3d 405, 93 Cal. Rptr. 338 (1971).

13. In Howard v. Bishop Byrne Council Home, 249 Md. 233, 241–42, 238 A. 2d 863, 868 (1969), the court upheld statutory charitable immunity: "We again restate our opinion that the General Assembly has completely investigated the immunity question, and the present statutes are tangible evidence that the legislature arrived at a solution which it deemed satisfactory."

14. In Haymes v. Catholic Bishop of Chicago, 41 Ill. 2d 366, 243 N.E. 2d 203 (1968), a $10,000 tort liability maximum limitation of recovery against private schools was found to be an arbitrary classification and invalid under the Illinois constitution.

15. Stern v. Lucy Webb Hayes National Training School for Deaconesses and Missionaries, 381 F. Supp. 1003 (D.D.C. 1974).

16. Analogous arguments have been raised in collective bargaining cases. The National Labor Relations Board has taken the position that because religious faculty take vows of poverty and obedience and stand in a different relationship with their employer than other employees, they have a "conflict of loyalties" and different economic

interests than other faculty and, therefore, do not have a "community of interest" with other employees. See, e.g., Seton Hill College, 201 NLRB 1026, 82 L.R.R.M. 1434 (1973), overruling Fordham University, 193 NLRB 134 (1971). The only two circuit courts which have reviewed this policy of the Board have rejected it. Niagara University v. NLRB, 558 F. 2d 1116 (2d Cir. 1977); NLRB v. St. Francis College, 562 F. 2d 246 (3d Cir. 1977).

17. This study makes no attempt to list the variety of ways in which a sponsoring religious body can exercise its influence and which again vary from jurisdiction to jurisdiction. Available at common law in some states, for example, is the power of visitation as an informal means to extend influence. "In essence, the power of visitation enables the founder of a charitable corporation to superintend and direct how and in what way the charity is to be administered so as to conform to the objectives for which it was founded." Fisch, Introduction, note 4 supra, p. 523.

18. For example, the General Board of the North Carolina Baptist Convention recently withheld $936,000 from Wake Forest University in a controversy over control of the university. *Chronicle of Higher Education*, Feb. 26, 1979, p. 2.

19. See Aiken and Porth, note 6 supra, and Knepper, Introduction, note 4 supra.

3. Public Financial Assistance

1. In a survey conducted by the Center for Constitutional Studies in conjunction with a study for the Sloan Commission on Government and Higher Education, 87 percent of the responding religiously affiliated colleges and universities indicated that they accepted some form of federal institutional assistance, and all admitted students who accepted some form of federal grant or loan. The combined institutional and student assistance in many instances amounted to a high percentage of the annual budgets of religiously affiliated institutions. "Government Regulation of Religiously Affiliated Higher Education," Study by the Center for Constitutional Studies, Notre Dame Law School, Notre Dame, Indiana, 1979, pp. 8–9.

2. Two colleges, Hillsdale College in Michigan and Grove City College in Pennsylvania, which have carefully avoided acceptance of institutional aid from the federal government, are currently engaged in litigation with the United States Department of HEW, testing the extent of the federal regulatory jurisdiction based solely upon the government aid to their students: In the matter of Hillsdale College and State of Michigan Administrative Proceeding in the Department of HEW, Docket No. A–7 (1978); Grove City College et al. v. Califano et al., Civil Action No. 78–1293, U.S. District Court, Western District of Pennsylvania (1978).

3. This brief summary of limitations by the states on public

funding relies almost entirely on the valuable and comprehensive work by A. E. Dick Howard, *State Aid to Private Higher Education* (Charlottesville, Va.: The Michie Company, 1977).

4. See, e.g., Ala. Const. art. IV, §93.

5. See, e.g., Almond v. Day, 199 Va. 1, 97 S.E. 2d 824 (1957).

6. Fort Sanders Presbyterian Hospital v. Health & Education Facilities Board, 224 Tenn. 240, 453 S.W. 2d 771 (1970).

7. Howard, note 3 supra, pp. 42–43.

8. Ibid., pp. 25–26.

9. S.C. Const. art. XI, §4.

10. See, e.g., College of New Rochelle v. Nyquist, 37 App. Div. 2d 461, 326 N.Y.S. 2d 765, 775 (1971).

11. Calif. Const. art. IX, 98; California Educational Facilities Auth. v. Priest, 116 Cal. Rptr. 361, 536 P. 2d 513, 519, note 8 (1974).

12. Wyo. Const. art. I, §19.

13. Utah Const. art. X, §13.

14. Howard, note 3 supra, p. 19.

15. Synod of South Dakota v. State, 2 S.D. 366, 50 N.W. 632 (1891).

16. Ohio Const. art. VI, §5.

17. Mass. Const. amend. art. XLVI, §2.

18. Texas Const. art III, §50b.

19. Ga. Const. art. VII, §1, par. 2(18).

20. Roemer v. Bd. of Public Works of Md., 426 U.S. 736 (1976), Hunt v. McNair, 413 U.S. 734 (1973); and Tilton v. Richardson, 403 U.S. 672 (1971).

21. Americans United for Separation of Church and State v. Blanton, 433 F. Supp. 97 (M.D. Tenn.), aff'd, 98 S. Ct. 39 (1977).

22. Id. at 100.

23. 403 U.S. at 686, accord Roemer, 426 U.S. at 755; see also Smith, 429 F. Supp. at 875, 877; and Americans United for Separation of Church and State v. Bubb, 387 F. Supp. 872 (D. Kans. 1974).

24. 403 U.S. at 615. Chief Justice Burger also noted that "[a]lthough only approximately 30 minutes a day are devoted to direct religious instruction, there are religiously oriented extracurricular activities." Ibid. See also Committee for Public Education and Religious Liberty v. Levitt, 342 F. Supp. 439, 440–41 (S.D.N.Y. 1972), aff'd, 413 U.S. 472 (1973); and Committee for Public Education and Religious Liberty v. Nyquist, 413 U.S. 756, 767 (1973), where the Court adopted a profile of sectarian nonpublic schools which included required attendance of pupils at religious activities.

25. See, e.g., Anderson v. Laird, 466 F. 2d 283 (D.C. Cir.), cert. denied, 409 U.S. 1076 (1972) (invalidating the compulsory chapel requirements for cadets at the service academies); School Dist. of Abington Twp. v. Schempp, 374 U.S. 203 (1963) (invalidating statutes providing for Bible reading or recitation of the Lord's Prayer in public schools, even though children could be excused at the request of a

parent); Engel v. Vitale, 370 U.S. 421 (1962) (invalidating the recitation of a "nondenominational" prayer in public schools).

26. Wrest v. Mt. Lebanon School District (Pa. C.P., Allegheny Co. 1974), as cited in American Jewish Congress, 18 *Litigation Docket of Pending Cases Affecting Freedom of Religion and Separation of Church and State* (hereinafter cited as AJC, *Docket*) 63 (1974) (sustaining a religious invocation and benediction by a clergyman at a high school commencement exercise on the theory that these prayers were "historical," serving for over sixty years a proper "secular purpose" in creating a serious and solemn atmosphere at an unofficial school function).

27. Balgooyen v. Los Gatos Joint Union High School District (Super. Ct. Cal. 1964) 4 AJC, *Docket* 24 (1966) (sustaining vesper-type baccalaureate services at a public high school on the ground that state involvement was minimal); see also Andrews v. Montour School District (Pa. C.P. 1968) 9 AJC, *Docket* 27 (1969) (accord; services conducted by religious groups involved, not by the school, and reasonable rental fee is paid to the school for the use of the facility).

28. See, e.g., Smith, 429 F. Supp. at 875; and see Moore v. Bd. of Ed. of Southwest School Dist. (Ohio C.P., Mercer Co. 1965), 4 AJC, *Docket* 29 (1966), and Petition of John J. Hopkins v. McWilliams (Tx. D. Ct., Kendall Co. 1966) 6 AJC, *Docket* 31 (1967).

29. 426 U.S. at 756.

30. Ibid.

4. Exercise of Religious Preference in Employment Policies

1. Manning M. Pattillo, Jr., and Donald M. MacKenzie, *Church-Sponsored Higher Education in the United States* (Washington, D.C.: American Council on Education, 1966), p. 50.

2. For a full report on the findings of this study, see *Government Regulation of Religiously Affiliated Higher Education*, a study prepared by the present authors for the Sloan Commission on Government and Higher Education, forthcoming.

3. Ibid., Chapter 2, p. 2.

4. Ibid., p. 3. Of those who exercise religious preference in the selection of their administrators, 29.7 percent indicated that the religious factor is decisive by itself, while the remaining 70.3 percent stated that it is one factor among many.

5. Ibid. Only 22.7 percent of those who exercise religious preference in faculty hiring indicated that the religious orientation or church membership of the applicant was decisive by itself in the selection process. The remaining 77.3 percent indicated that this factor is considered as one among many.

6. Ibid. Of those who exercise religious preference in the selection of nonteaching staff, very few (3.3 percent) indicated that the religious

orientation or church membership of a prospective staff employee is decisive by itself; 23 percent indicated that the religious factor is one among many; and 3.8 percent stated that this factor is not very important.

7. "Achieving the Mission of Church-Related Institutions of Higher Learning," Report of a conference held Nov. 29–30, 1976 (Washington, D.C.: Association of American Colleges, 1977), pp. 6–7.

8. James Tunstead Burtchaell, C.S.C., "Sermon at Mass Inaugurating the Academic Year," Sept. 10, 1972, as cited in *Notre Dame Report*, No. 1 (1972–73), pp. 51–52.

9. See Moots and Gaffney, note 2 supra, Chapter 11.

10. For an excellent review of state provisions concerning eligibility for public financial assistance, see A. E. Dick Howard, *State Aid to Private Higher Education* (Charlottesville, Va.: Michie Publishing Co., 1977).

11. See, e.g., Grove City College v. Califano (W. D. Pa., Civil Action No. 78–1293, filed Nov. 22, 1978).

12. See, e.g., The Higher Education Facilities Act of 1963, as amended, 20 U.S.C. 711–21; other examples of institutional assistance would include research contracts with various federal agencies such as the Departments of Defense, Justice (LEAA) and Health, Education and Welfare.

13. See, e.g., the Guaranteed Student Loan Program, Title IV-B of the Higher Education Act of 1965, as amended, 20 U.S.C. 1071; the Basic Educational Opportunity Grants (BEOG), Title IX-A-1 of the Higher Education Act of 1965, as amended, 20 U.S.C. 1078; and the Veterans' Education Benefits (G.I. Bill), 38 U.S.C. chapters 31, 34, 35, and 36.

14. 402 U.S. 672 (1971).

15. "Rather than focus on the four defendant colleges and universities involved in this case, however, appellants seek to shift our attention to a 'composite profile' they have constructed of the 'typical sectarian' institution of higher education. . . . Individual projects can be properly evaluated if and when challenges arise with respect to particular recipients and some evidence is then presented to show that the institution does in fact possess [such] characteristics [as to make it ineligible for aid]. We cannot, however, strike down an Act of Congress on the basis of a hypothetical 'profile.'" Id. at 682.

16. Id. at 684.

17. Id. at 686, 687.

18. 413 U.S. 734 (1973).

19. The college was controlled by the South Carolina Baptist Convention to the extent that the church convention elected all members of the college's board of trustees, and the church retained the power to approve certain financial transactions and amendments of the college's charter. Id. at 743.

20. Ibid.

21. 426 U.S. 736 (1976).

22. After *Tilton* the Maryland statute was amended to provide "None of the moneys payable under this subtitle shall be utilized by the institutions for sectarian purposes." Maryland Laws of 1972, chapter 534 as cited in *Roemer*, 426 U.S. at 740–41. Compliance with this provision is insured by administration of the grant program by the Council for Higher Education, which both determines whether an institution applying for aid is eligible at all and requires that institutions that are eligible for funds do not put them to any sectarian use. Id. at 741–42.

23. Id. at 759, citing the District Court opinion, 387 F. Supp. 1282, 1293 (D. Md. 1974).

24. 426 U.S. at 761, referring to *Hunt*, 413 U.S. at 744, and *Tilton* 403 U.S. at 682, but ignoring the Court's acceptance of such composite profiles in cases involving elementary and secondary schools; see, e.g., Committee for Public Education and Religious Liberty v. Nyquist, 413 U.S. 756 (1973); Levitt v. Committee for Public Education, 413 U.S. 472 (1973); and Lemon v. Kurtzman, 403 U.S. 602 (1971).

25. 403 U.S. 602 (1971) (invalidating a Rhode Island and a Pennsylvania scheme whereby the state purchased the services of instructors of secular subjects in nonpublic elementary and secondary schools). In Committee for Public Education and Religious Liberty v. Nyquist, 413 U.S. 756, 768 (1973), Justice Powell accepted verbatim from the appellant's brief the contention that religiously affiliated schools in New York placed religious restrictions on faculty appointments. Religious preference in faculty hiring did not, however, become an issue for decision or comment in a subsequent case involving an Ohio statute providing for various forms of aid to students at nonpublic elementary and secondary schools, for the parties stipulated that none of the schools covered by the statute practiced discrimination in faculty hiring on the basis of race, creed, color, or national origin. Wolman v. Walter, 433 U.S. 299, 234–35 (1977); see also Wolman v. Essex, 417 F. Supp. 1113, 1116 (N.D. Ohio 1976).

26. 426 U.S. at 749, citing *Lemon*, 403 U.S. at 618; see also 426 U.S. at 752, note 18.

27. Id. at 757, referring to 387 F. Supp. at 1294.

28. The Grove City College case, referred to in note 11 above, presents a challenge to the exercise of federal jurisdiction over a college which does not receive any direct institutional assistance from the federal government and which administers only those forms of federally assisted student aid programs which in the college's view are nondiscretionary in character.

In Bob Jones University v. Johnson, 396 F. Supp. 597 (D.S.C. 1975), aff'd. per curiam, 529 F. 2d 514 (4th Cir. 1975), the courts sustained a ruling of the Veterans' Administration terminating the university's eligibility to enroll students who receive federal assistance under the G.I. Bill. The district court held that by enrolling such students, the university was receiving federal financial assistance within the meaning of Title VI of the Civil Rights Act of 1964 and was therefore subject to the strictures of the act. See also Norwood v. Harrison, 413 U.S. 455 (1973); Brown v. South Carolina Bd. of Ed., 296 F. Supp. 199 (D.S.C. 1968), aff'd per curiam, 393 U.S. 222 (1968); and Poindexter v. Louisiana Financial Assistance Commission, 275 F. Supp. 833 (E.D. La. 1967), aff'd per curiam, 389 U.S. 571 (1968) (invalidating state textbook loans and tuition grants in the context of racially segregated private elementary and secondary schools.

It is not clear what a court would do in the context of a conflict with the government over religious preference in a federally funded program. But it should be noted that the government's refusal to support programs which involve invidious racial and gender-based discrimination rests on more solid constitutional footing and has clearer statutory authority than would a policy which could infringe against the Free Exercise Clause by denying to a religious group the right to exercise religious preference in positions directly related to the mission or goal of the religious body.

29. 429 F. Supp. 871 (W.D.N.C.), summarily aff'd., 434 U.S. 803 (1977).

30. 429 F. Supp. at 874.

31. Id. at 876. See also Americans United for Separation of Church and State v. Bubb, 379 F. Supp. 872, 880–81 (D. Kan. 1974).

32. 429 F. Supp. at 878.

33. 433 F. Supp. 97 (M.D. Tenn.), summarily aff'd., 434 U.S. 803 (1977).

34. 433 F. Supp. at 100 (emphasis added).

35. See, e.g., Wolman v. Walter, 433 U.S. 229 (1977) (sustaining loan of secular textbooks by state to all children, whether attending public, private, or parochial elementary and secondary schools); Meek v. Pittenger, 421 U.S. 349 (1975) (same); Bd. of Ed. v. Allen, 392 U.S. 236 (1968) (same); and Everson v. Bd. of Ed., 330 U.S. 1 (1947) (sustaining state program of reimbursement of student bus fares to parents of children attending elementary and secondary schools, regardless of the character of the school). The last three cases are discussed by the *Blanton* court, 433 F. Supp. at 102.

36. 413 U.S. 756 (1973), discussed in *Blanton*, 433 F. Supp. at 101–3.

37. 433 F. Supp. at 100 (emphasis added).

38. See, e.g., Tully v. Griffin, Inc., 429 U.S. 68, 74 (1976); Hicks v. Miranda, 422 U.S. 332, 343–45 (1975); Ohio ex rel. Eaton v. Price, 360 U.S. 246, 247 (1959). And see Robert L. Stern and Eugene Gressman, *Supreme Court Practice* (Washington, D.C.: Bureau of National Affairs, 5th ed. 1978), pp. 321–25; and Charles Alan Wright, *Law of Federal Courts* (St. Paul: West Publishing Co., 3d ed. 1976), pp. 550–51.

39. Justices Brennan, Marshall, and Stevens voted in both *Smith* and *Blanton* to schedule the cases for oral argument and plenary review.

40. If either *Smith* or *Blanton* had involved evidence of a practice of religious preference in all positions of employment, one might reasonably speculate that this factor alone may have persuaded another justice to join Justices Brennan, Marshall, and Stevens to provide the fourth vote needed for plenary review, and that the outcome of the case may have been different.

41. Edelman v. Jordan, 415 U.S. 651, 671 (1974); and Colorado Springs Amusements, Ltd. v. Rizzo, 428 U.S. 913 (1976) (Brennan, J., dissenting from denial of certiorari). And see Note, "Summary Dispositions of Supreme Court Appeals: The Significance of Limited Discretion and a Theory of Limited Precedent," 52 *Bos. U.L. Rev.* 373 (1972). In his treatise on the law of federal courts, Professor Wright observes that since "in most cases the Court summarily affirms . . . for want of a substantial federal question, . . . they are of scant comfort to the appellant who has obtained no relief." Wright, note 38 supra, p. 551.

42. "The term, 'employer' means a person engaged in an industry affecting commerce who has fifteen or more employees in the current or preceding calendar year, and any agent of such a person." Pub. L. 88–352, Title VII, §701 (b), July 2, 1964, 78 Stat. 253, 42 U.S.C. 2000e as amended by Pub. L. 92–261, §2, Mar. 2, 1972, 86 Stat. 103. The original provision in the 1964 act covered employers with twenty-five or more employees, but the reach of Title VII was extended in 1972 by an amendment defining covered employers as those with fifteen or more employees.

43. In the legislative history of the Civil Rights Act of 1964, there is ample evidence of congressional intent to rely also on the enforcement clause of the Fourteenth Amendment, but when the Supreme Court sustained the Civil Rights Act of 1964, it grounded its decision solely on the Commerce Clause. See Heart of Atlanta Motel v. United States, 379 U.S. 241 (1964).

44. "It shall be an unlawful employment practice for an employer (1) to fail or refuse to hire or to discharge any individual, or otherwise to discriminate against any individual with respect to his compensation, terms, conditions, or privileges or employment, because of such individual's race, color, religion, sex, or national origin; or (2) to limit, segregate, or classify his employee or applicants for employment in any way which would deprive or tend to deprive any individual of employment opportunities or otherwise adversely affect his status as an employee, because of such individual's race, color, religion, sex, or national origin." Pub. L. 88–352, Title VII, §703 (a), 78 Stat. 255, 42 U.S.C. 2000e–2 (a).

45. If any institution accepted federal funds, however, it was subject to the provisions of Title VI of the 1964 act, which states: "No person in the United States shall, on the ground of race, color, or national origin, be excluded from participation in, be denied the benefits of, or be subjected to discrimination under any program or activity receiving Federal financial assistance." Pub. L. 88–352, Title VI, §601,

78 Stat. 252, 42 U.S.C. 2000d. See United States by Clark v. Frazer, 297 F. Supp. 319 (D. Ala. 1968).

46. If an educational institution accepted federal funds, however, after June 23, 1972 it became subject to the provisions of Title IX of the Education Amendments of 1972, which states: "No person in the United States shall, on the basis of sex, be excluded from participation in, be denied the benefits of, or be subjected to discrimination under any education program or activity receiving Federal financial assistance. . . ." Noting the more specific focus of this provision on access to federally funded educational programs, several district courts have invalidated administrative regulations issued by HEW concerning the employment policies of federally funded educational programs. Romeo Community Schools v. HEW, 438 F. Supp. 1021 (E.D. Mich. 1977), McCarthy v. Burkholder, 448 F. Supp. 41 (D. Kan. 1978), and Brunswick School Bd. v. Califano, 449 F. Supp. 866 (D. Me. 1978).

47. For the remarks of Senator Humphrey, see 110 *Cong. Rec.* 12722 (June 4, 1964), reprinted in Bernard Schwartz, ed., *Statutory History of the United States: Civil Rights* (New York: McGraw-Hill, 1970), p. 1349. For the remarks of Senator Dirksen, see 110 *Cong. Rec.* 12817 (June 5, 1964), reprinted in Schwartz, p. 1361.

48. 110 *Cong. Rec.* 12722; Schwartz, p. 1349.

49. Remarks of Sen. Harrison Williams, Feb. 1, 1972, as cited in U.S. Senate, Committee on Labor and Public Welfare, *Legislative History of the Equal Employment Opportunity Act of 1972 (H.R. 1746, Pub. L. 92–261)* (Washington, D.C.: Government Printing Office: 1972), p. 1252; see also remarks of Sen. Jacob Javits, ibid., pp. 1253–54.

50. Pub. L. 88–352, 78 Stat. 255, as amended by Pub. L. 92–261, 86 Stat. 103, 42 U.S.C. 2000e–1.

51. See *Legislative History*, note 49 supra, pp. 849–53.

52. Ibid., pp. 843–49, 1216–17, 1227–31.

53. Ibid., p. 844.

54. Amendment No. 809 to S.2515, ibid., p. 789.

55. Ibid., pp. 848–49.

56. Ibid., p. 850.

57. Ibid., p. 1667.

58. Ibid., pp. 1813–14.

59. Amendment No. 815 to S. 2515, ibid., p. 881.

60. Ibid., p. 1227.

61. Ibid., pp. 1223, 1229.

62. Ibid., pp. 1223, 1229.

63. Ibid., p. 1251.

64. Among the Christian groups opposed to the amendment were the National Council of Churches and the U.S. Catholic Conference, and agencies of the American Baptist Church, the Episcopal Church, the Lutheran Church in America, the United Church of Christ, the United Methodist Church, and the United Presbyterian Church. Among Jewish groups opposed to the amendment were the American Jewish Commit-

tee, the American Jewish Congress, the Anti-defamation League of B'nai B'rith, Hadassah, and the United Synagogue of America. Ibid., p. 1253.

65. Ibid., pp. 1259–60.

66. Pub. L. 88–352, Title VII, §703 (e) (1), 78 Stat. 256, 42 U.S.C. 2000e–2 (e) (1).

67. H. R. Rep. No. 88, 88th Cong., 1st Sess. (1963), as cited in Bernard Schwartz, ed., note 47 supra, p. 1074.

68. 110 *Cong. Rec.* 2585 (Feb. 8, 1964).

69. Id. at 2586 (Feb. 8, 1964).

70. Ibid.

71. In support of this view, for example, Congressman Albert Quie argued: "I think there is no way for the Federal Government to make a proper decision as to the religion of employees in religious education institutions. . . . Just to make it abundantly clear, in the case of religious educational institutions or those that propagate a particular religion, they can have this freedom to decide whether they think a janitor or somebody to take care of their lawns or a mathematics professor or someone working in the treasurer's office in the college or any other employee should be of any particular religion. They may want him to be of their own religion or of some other religion. I think we had better leave religious decisions to religious institutions themselves and not attempt to do it through Federal executive agencies." Quie evidently felt that this latitude of discretion by religiously affiliated colleges could not be affectuated by the BFOQ exception, for he concluded his remarks: "Therefore I believe we can and should support [the Purcell] amendment." Id. at 2590. See also the remarks of Congressman Harris, id. at 2586.

72. In opposition to the Purcell amendment, for example, Congressman Gill argued: "If what is involved is the control of the institution or exercising guidance over it, as some of your boards of visitors in your Methodist colleges do, fine; you are exempted in the act. It is a bona fide condition of employment. But if it is a matter of working as a janitor or cafeteria employee, why should you be a Methodist, Presbyterian, Catholic, or, in my state [Hawaii], a Buddhist? What difference does it make as long as you can do the job? I might ask you further what difference does religion make to a mathematics professor at Southern Methodist? Are Methodists better mathematics professors than Presbyterians or Baptists? Not necessarily. It depends on the individual." Id. at 2590. See also the remarks of Congressman McCulloch, id. at 2587.

73. Barbara Lindemann Schlei and Paul Grossman, *Employment Discrimination Law* (Washington, D.C.: Bureau of National Affairs, 1976), pp. 292–93.

74. Kent M. Weeks, "Religious Preference in Faculty and Staff Employment," paper delivered to the First Annual Conference on Legal Problems in Independent Higher Education, Notre Dame, Indiana, Oct. 18, 1978, p. 13.

75. On the value of committee reports and legislative debates as extrinsic aids to determine legislative intent, see Dallas Sands, ed., *Sutherland Statutes and Statutory Construction* (Chicago: Callaghan, 4th ed., 1973), §48.06, pp. 203-5, and §§48.13-48.15, pp. 216-22.

76. Pub. L. 88-352, Title VII, §703 (e) (2), 78 Stat. 255, 42 U.S.C. 2000e-2 (e) (2).

77. 110 *Cong. Rec.* 2590 (Feb. 8, 1964). In a similar vein Congressman Gary noted that his support for the Purcell amendment arose in part from his experience as a member of the board of trustees of a large Baptist college which "employs Negroes" but which on his view ought not "to be forced to employ a janitor or any other employee who is . . . a member of some other religious faith unless it wishes to do so." Id. at 2592.

78. Id. at 2585.

79. See, e.g., the remarks of Congressmen Quie and Gary referred to above in note 77.

80. 460 F. 2d 553 (5th Cir.), cert. denied, 409 U.S. 896 (1972).

81. Watson v. Jones, 80 U.S. (13 Wall.) 679 (1872) (regarding the decisions of the highest church judicatories on questions of discipline, faith, or ecclesiastical rule as final and binding on civil courts).

82. 460 F. 2d at 560. See also Presbyterian Church v. Mary Elizabeth Blue Hull Presbyterian Church, 393 U.S. 440 (1969). In Blue Hull the Court stated: "First Amendment values are plainly jeopardized when church property litigation is made to turn on the resolution by civil courts of controversies over religious doctrine and practice. If civil courts undertake to resolve such controversies in order to adjudicate the property dispute, the hazards are ever present of inhibiting the free development of religious doctrine and of implicating secular interests in matters of purely ecclesiastical concern. . . . The Amendment therefore commands civil courts to decide church property disputes without resolving underlying controversies over religious doctrines." Id. at 449.

83. Id. at 560-61.

84. 498 F. 2d 51 (D.C. Cir.), cert. denied, 419 U.S. 996 (1974); see Note, "The constitutionality of the 1972 Amendment to Title VII's Exemption for Religious Organizations," 73 *Mich. L. Rev.* 538 (1973).

85. In re Complaint by Anderson, 34 FCC 2d 937, 938 (1972).

86. 47 CFR 73.125(a), 73.3301(a), 73.599(a), 73.680(a), 73.793 (a) (Oct. 1, 1973); see also Non-Discrimination in Employment Practices: Notice of Proposed Rule Making, 13 FCC 2d 240 (1969).

87. 498 F. 2d at 53.

88. Ibid.

89. Id. at 55.

90. Ibid.

91. Id. at 57.

92. Ibid.

93. Id. at 57-58. The Commission exempted from the ban on sectarian hiring "the employment of persons whose work is . . . connected with the espousal of the licensee's religion." Id. at 59.

94. Id. at 61 (Bazelon, Chief Judge, concurring).

95. 419 U.S. 996 (1974). Denial of certiorari cannot, of course, be construed as a ruling by the Supreme Court on the merits of the case, but only as notice that fewer than four members of the Court wished to hear the case. Hughes Tool Co. v. TWA, 409 U.S. 363, 365 n. 1 (1973); Brown v. Allen, 344 U.S. 443, 489–97 (1953); Maryland v. Baltimore Radio Show, 338 U.S. 912 (1950) (opinion of Frankfurter, J.).

96. 406 U.S. 205 (1972).

97. EEOC Decision No. 75-186 (Feb. 21, 1975).

98. 29 CFR §1606.1 (a), issued Jan. 13, 1970, provides: "The Commission is aware of the widespread practices of discrimination on the basis of national origin, and intends to apply the full force of law to eliminate such discrimination. The bona fide occupational qualification exception as it pertains to national origin cases shall be strictly construed."

99. 29 CFR §1604.2 (a), issued Apr. 5, 1972, provides:

> The Commission believes that the bona fide occupational qualification exception as to sex should be interpreted narrowly. Labels—'men's jobs' and 'women's jobs'—tend to deny employment opportunities unnecessarily to one sex or the other.
>
> (1) The Commission will find that the following situations do not warrant the application of the bona fide occupational qualification exception:
>
> (i) The refusal to hire a woman because of her sex based on assumptions of the comparative employment characteristics of women in general. For example, the assumption that the turnover rate among women is higher than among men.
>
> (ii) The refusal to hire an individual based on stereotyped characterizations of the sexes. Such stereotypes include, for example, that men are less capable of assembling intricate equipment; that women are less capable of aggressive salesmanship. The principle of nondiscrimination requires that individuals be considered on the basis of individual capacities and not on the basis of any characteristics generally attributed to the group.
>
> (iii) The refusal to hire an individual because of the preferences of co-workers, the employer, clients or customers except as covered specifically in subparagraph (2) of this paragraph.
>
> . . .
>
> (2) Where it is necessary for the purpose of authenticity or genuineness, the Commission will consider sex to be a bona fide occupational qualification, e.g., an actor or actress.

See also Diaz v. Pan American Airways, 442 F. 2d 385 (5th Cir.) cert. denied, 404 U.S. 950 (1971).

100. See, e.g., Dothard v. Rawlinson, 433 U.S. 321, 334 (1977); McDonald v. Santa Fe Trail Transportation Co., 427 U.S. 273, 279–80 (1976); Griggs v. Duke Power Co., 401 U.S. 424, 434 (1971).

101. 29 CFR 1605.1, issued July 13, 1967.

102. The Senate adopted this amendment by a vote of 55 to 0. For

the floor debate concerning this amendment, see 118 *Cong. Rec.* 705-31 (Jan. 21, 1972). The lawsuit which provoded this legislative response was Dewey v. Reynolds Metals Co., 429 F. 2d 324 (6th Cir. 1970), aff'd. by equally divided Court, 402 U.S. 689 (1971); but see Riley v. Bendix Corp. 464 F. 2d 1113 (5th Cir. 1972).

103. 432 U.S. 63 (1977).

104. Executive Order 11246 was signed by President Johnson on Sept. 24, 1965; it was amended by Executive Order 11375, signed by President Johnson on Oct. 13, 1967, to add sex as a prohibited basis of discrimination. Amended Part I of the Order, dealing with nondiscrimination in employment by the federal government, was superseded by Executive Order 11478, signed by President Nixon on Aug. 8, 1969.

105. Id.

106. Executive Order 11246, 202 (1) and (2).

107. See, e.g., testimony of the Rev. James T. Burtchaell, C.S.C., then Provost of the University of Notre Dame, before the Department of Labor, Washington, D.C., Oct. 1, 1975.

108. 41 CFR 60-1.5 (a) (5), as amended at 40 F.R. 13218 (Mar. 25, 1975).

109. 41 CFR 60-50.1 (2), as amended at 40 F.R. 13218 (Mar. 25, 1975).

110. Rev. Rul. 71-447, citing Restatement (Second) of Trusts §377 (1959), Comment C: "A trust for a purpose the accomplishment of which is contrary to public policy, although not forbidden by law, is invalid."

111. For example, Title VI of the Civil Rights Act of 1964, P.L. 88-352, 78 Stat. 241, 42 U.S.C. 2000c-6 and 2000d explicitly prohibit racial discrimination in federally funded educational programs. Furthermore, this provision may be regarded as a statutory extension of the constitutionally based policy announced by the Supreme Court in Brown v. Bd. of Education, 347 U.S. 483 (1954).

112. Rev. Proc. 75-50 §4.07, 1975-2 C.B. 587.

113. A. E. Dick Howard, *State Aid to Private Higher Education.*

114. New York Constitution, art. XI, §3; see Howard, pp. 609-38.

115. See, e.g., Application of Iona College, 65 Misc. 2d 329, 316 N.Y.S. 2d 139 (Sup. Ct. Albany County 1970); College of New Rochelle v. Nyquist, 37 App. Div. 2d 461, 326 N.Y.S. 2d 765 (3d Dept. 1971); and Canisius College v. Nyquist, 36 App. Div. 2d 340, 320 N.Y.S. 2d 652 (3d Dept. 1971).

116. New York Constitution, art. I, §11 [emphasis supplied].

117. Council of the State Governments, *Suggested State Legislation,* Vol. 26 (1967).

118. Ann. Code of Md. art. 49 B, sec. 20.

119. Minn. Laws Ann. sec. 363.02; Ky. Rev. Stat. 344.090(A); Ann. Code of Md. art. 49B, sec. 19 (g) (1); Pa. Stat. Ann. sec. 5 (a); Hawaii Stat. sec. 378-9 (2); 25 Okla. Stat. Ann. Title 25 sec. 1308; Ill. Ann. Stat. sec. 853 (e) (2); Ann. Laws of Mass. C 151 B, sec. 4-1.

120. Ind. Code 22-9-1-3 (h); Minn. Laws Ann. 363.01 subd. 21;

Rev. Stat. sec. 344.090 (3); Ann. Code of Md. art. 49B, sec. 19 (g) (2); 25 Okla. Stat. Ann. Title 25, sec. 1306 (2).

5. Academic Freedom

1. The American Association of University Professors (AAUP) maintains a standing committee (Committee A) to police the implementation of the Association's statements on academic freedom and tenure and academic due process. If the investigators appointed by this Committee find evidence of serious infractions of the principles enunciated in the AAUP statements, they can recommend that the full committee impose various kinds of sanctions, including censure, on administrations found to be deficient in this respect. Of the forty-five institutions listed in the December 1978 issue of the AAUP Bulletin as censured administrations, only nine are related to a religious body. *AAUP Bulletin* 64 (1978) p. 285. Of these nine institutions, some had a historical link with a religious body in the past but currently maintain only a nominal connection with the religious body. See, e.g., "Grove City College," *AAUP Bulletin* 49 (1963), 15–24. On the other hand, at least one public institution was censured not only at a single campus but throughout an entire system of state community colleges. See "The Virginia Community College System," *AAUP Bulletin* 61 (1975), 30–38. It would be misleading, therefore, to conclude from the raw data contained in the most recent AAUP list of censured administrations that 20 percent of these institutions are religiously affiliated. For the current status of administrations censured by the AAUP, see "Developments Relating to Censure by the Association," *AAUP Bulletin* 64 (1978), 99–107, and "Report of Committee A, 1977–78," *AAUP Bulletin* 64 (1978), 166–72.

2. See, e.g., "University of Detroit," *AAUP Bulletin* 63 (1978), 36–54.

3. For examples of disputes of this character over academic freedom at religiously affiliated colleges, see "Marquette University," *AAUP Bulletin* 62 (1976), 83–94; "Concordia Seminary (Missouri)," ibid., 61 (1975), 49–59; "St. Mary's College (Minnesota)," ibid., 54 (1968), 37–42; "St. John's University (New York)," ibid., 52 (1966), 12–19; "Livingstone College," ibid., 43 (1957), 188–99.

4. It is difficult to interpret these data because no precise definition of "religious preference" was articulated in the survey instrument. Thus some respondents may have understood the phrase to refer only to membership, including nominal affiliation, in a religious body, while others may have understood religious preference to include the actual practices and beliefs of professors being considered for tenure. Of those who stated that they exercise religious preference in the tenure decision, 15.4 percent indicated that the religious factor is decisive by itself; 78.8 percent stated that this factor was one among many, and 5.8 percent indicated that the religious factor was not very important. Thirty-three (18 percent) of the respondents cited an official

policy or their personal opinion in support of the exercise of religious preference in granting tenure to their faculty members.

5. *Academic Excellence and Professional Growth: The Tenure Policy of William Jewell College* (Liberty, Mo., 1976), p. 8.

6. 403 U.S. 672, 681 (1971).

7. Ibid.

8. Id. at 681–82.

9. 413 U.S. 734, 743 (1973).

10. 426 U.S. 736, 756 (1976).

11. Ibid., note 20.

12. 426 U.S. at 773 (Stewart, J., dissenting).

13. 403 U.S. at 686.

14. Id. at 687.

15. 433 F. Supp. 97 (M.D. Tenn.) summarily aff'd., 434 U.S. 803 (1977).

16. 433 F. Supp. at 100 (emphasis supplied).

17. 429 F. Supp. 871 (W.D. N.C.) summarily aff'd., 434 U.S. 803 (1977).

18. 429 F. Supp. at 875, 877.

19. See, however, the editorial written by Charles M. Whelan, S.J., "Free Choice for College Students," *America* 137 (Oct. 22, 1977), 257.

20. See, e.g., the comments of Derek Bok, President of Harvard University, and of Kingman Brewster, then President of Yale University, reported in Introduction, note 3 supra.

21. See, e.g., Chapter 11 in the forthcoming volume prepared by the present authors as a report to the Sloan Commission on Government and Higher Education.

22. The case involves Regis College in Denver, Colorado. See Robert Jacobson's report of the lawsuit in the *Chronicle of Higher Education*, Mar. 5, 1979, p. 13.

23. See, e.g., Meyer v. Nebraska, 262 U.S. 390 (1923) (invalidating a prohibition against the teaching of German in public elementary and secondary schools), and Epperson v. Arkansas, 393 U.S. 97 (1968) (invalidating an "anti-evolution statute" which prohibited the teaching of the theory that man evolved from other species of life). And see Hendren v. Campbell, 45 L.W. 2530 (Superior Ct. Ind. May 17, 1977) (prohibiting use in public school of a facially neutral biology textbook the purpose of which was "the promotion and inclusion of fundamentalist Christian doctrines").

24. See, e.g., Pierce v. Society of Sisters, 268 U.S. 510 (1925) (invalidating a state statute requiring attendance at public schools); and see Wisconsin v. Yoder, 406 U.S. 205 (1972) (invalidating under the Free Exercise Clause a compulsory school attendance law as applied to Amish children who had completed the eighth grade of elementary school instruction).

25. Contrast, e.g., Adler v. Bd. of Education, 342 U.S. 495 (1952) (upholding the New York Feinberg Law and other loyalty regulations for teachers), with Wieman v. Updegraff, 344 U.S. 183 (1952) (in-

validating as overbroad an Oklahoma loyalty oath challenged by faculty members at a state college). In Keyishian v. Bd. of Regents, 385 U.S. 589 (1967), the Court overturned Adler.

26. Contrast, Sweezy v. New Hampshire, 354 U.S. 234 (1957) (invalidating the conviction of a teacher at a state college who refused to testify to the State Attorney General about the contents of a lecture on socialism), with Barenblatt v. United States, 360 U.S. 109 (1959) (congressional power to investigate alleged Communist activities "is not to be denied solely because the field of education is involved").

27. See, e.g., Shelton v. Tucker, 364 U.S. 479 (1960) (invalidating as overbroad a requirement that teachers list all organizational affiliations).

28. See Thomas I. Emerson, *The System of Freedom of Expression* (New York: Random House, 1970), pp. 611–16.

29. 354 U.S. 234 (1957).

30. Id. at 250; see also Keyishian v. Bd. of Regents, 385 U.S. 589 (1967).

31. Among groups to which the Supreme Court has extended the constitutional protection of freedom of association are civil rights groups (NAACP v. Alabama ex rel. Patterson, 357 U.S. 449 [1958]), political parties (Buckley v. Valeo, 424 U.S. 1 [1976]), labor organizations (United Transportation Union v. Michigan, 401 U.S. 576 [1971]), and corporations (First National Bank of Boston v. Bellotti, 435 U.S. 765 [1978]).

32. See, e.g., Healy v. James, 408 U.S. 169, 180 (1972).

33. See, e.g., Browzin v. Catholic University of America, 527 F. 2d 843 (D.C. Cir. 1975), noted in 62 *Iowa L. Rev.* 509 (1976).

34. W. Todd Furniss, "The Status of 'AAUP Policy,'" *Ed, Record* 59 (1978), 7–29.

35. Ralph S. Brown, Jr., and Matthew W. Finkin, "The Usefulness of AAUP Policy," *Ed Record* 59 (1978), 30–44.

36. American Association of University Professors, *Policy Documents and Reports* (Washington, D.C.: American Association of University Professors, 1977). The 1940 statement is printed regularly in the professional magazine of the Association; see, e.g., *AAUP Bulletin* 64 (1978), 108–12.

37. But see Abbariao v. Hamline University School of Law, 258 N.W. 2d 108 (Minn. 1977). On the elusive concept of "state action," regarded by at least one constitutional scholar as "anti-doctrine," see Laurence H. Tribe, *American Constitutional Law* (Mineola, N.Y.: Foundation Press, 1978), pp. 1147–74.

38. For a statement of the societal values protected by the First Amendment, see Thomas I. Emerson, *Toward a General Theory of the First Amendment* (New York: Random House, 1963), p. 3. For a statement of the core values underlying procedural due process in American law, see Tribe, supra note 37, pp. 502–4.

39. See, e.g., Deut. 16:18–20; 17:8–13; Amos 5:7, 10–13; Prov. 17:15, 23; Dan. 13:28–59; Matt. 18:15–18.

40. See, e.g., Theodore M. Hesburgh, C.S.C., *The Humane Imperative:*

A Challenge for the Year 2000 (New Haven: Yale University Press, 1974), pp. 79, 82–83.

41. Such a posture by a college affiliated with the Roman Catholic communion would appear to violate the teaching of the Second Vatican Council: "This Vatican Synod declares that the human person has a right to religious freedom. This freedom means that all men are to be immune from coercion on the part of individuals or of social groups and of any human power, in such wise that in matters religious no one is to be forced to act in a manner contrary to his own beliefs. Nor is anyone to be restrained from acting in accordance with his own beliefs, whether privately or publicly, whether alone or in association with others, within due limits." *Declaration on Religious Freedom*, par. 2, in Walter Abbott and Joseph Gallagher, eds., *The Documents of Vatican II* (New York: Herder and Herder, 1966), pp. 678–79. For the teaching of other Christian communions on religious freedom, see A. F. Carrillo de Albornoz, *The Basis of Religious Liberty* (Geneva: World Council of Churches, 1963).

42. When Chief Justice Burger drew the line in *Tilton* between institutions which are eligible and those which are ineligible to receive public assistance, it is noteworthy that he employed the term "proselytize," for the distinction between witness and proselytism is well known in Christian literature on missiology, and is used to exalt the former and to condemn the latter for its use of coercive tactics in eliciting "belief." This concern was reflected in the debates of the Second Vatican Council. See, e.g., Werner Becker, "History of the Decree on Ecumenism," in Herbert Vorgrimler, ed., *Commentary on the Documents of Vatican II* (New York: Herder and Herder, 1968), Vol. 2, p. 53. And the Ecumenical Directory issued by the Congregation for Promoting Christian Unity expressly states that "care should be taken to avoid any suspicion of proselytism" (Art. 46), as cited in ibid., p. 107.

6. Student Admissions and Student Discipline

1. *AAPICU* [American Association of Presidents of Independent Colleges and Universities] *Report*, April 1976, p. 8.

2. See, e.g., Steward Machine Co. v. Davis, 301 U.S. 548 (1937) (sustaining the unemployment compensation provisions of the Social Security Act under the Taxing and Spending Clause); NLRB v. Jones and Laughlin Steel Corp., 301 U.S. 1 (1937) (sustaining the regulation of labor relations under the Commerce Clause).

3. For the legislative history of this act, see Bernard Schwartz, ed., *Statutory History of the United States: Civil Rights* (New York: McGraw-Hill, 1970), vol. 2, pp. 1017–1452. For the Supreme Court decision upholding the act, see Heart of Atlanta Motel v. United States, 379 U.S. 241 (1964).

4. See Title IX of the Education Amendments of 1972, Pub. L. 92-318, 86 Stat. 373, 20 U.S.C. 1681 et seq., and section 504 of the Vocational Rehabilitation Act of 1973, Pub. L. 93-112, 87 Stat. 361, 29 U.S.C. 794.

5. Marchetti v. United States, 390 U.S. 39 (1968).

6. National League of Cities v. Usery, 426 U.S. 833 (1976).

7. See the forthcoming volume by the present authors on governmental regulation of church related higher education.

8. Francis C. Gamelin, *Towards a Master Plan* (Washington, D.C.: Lutheran Education Conference of North America, 1978).

9. Garry A. Greinke, *Survival with a Purpose: A Master Plan Revisited* (Washington, D.C.: Lutheran Education Conference of North America, 1978), p. 63.

10 403 U.S. 672, 682 (1971).

11. Id. at 686.

12. See, e.g., Bd. of Ed. v. Allen, 392 U.S. 236 (1968); Committee for Public Education and Religious Liberty v. Nyquist, 413 U.S. 756, 813 (1973) (White, J., dissenting).

13. 403 U.S. 661, 671, n.2.

14. See, e.g., Wolman v. Walter, where the parties stipulated that "none of the schools covered by the statute discriminate in the admission of pupils or in the hiring of teachers on the bases of race, *creed*, color or national origin." 433 U.S. 229, 234–35 (1977) (emphasis supplied).

15. 413 U.S. 734, 743 (1973).

16. Id. at 743–44 (emphasis supplied) (citation omitted).

17. Id. at 744.

18. As is true with several public funding cases recently, in *Roemer* it is important to attend carefully to the mathematics of the opinions. Justices White and Rehnquist clearly agreed with the result reached by the Court and would probably have been more expansive if they had the support of a majority for their views. In this sense only does Justice Blacmun's opinion reflect that of a majority. As it is, only three other justices joined in Justice Blackmun's opinion.

19. 426 U.S. 736, 755 (1976).

20. Id. at 757–58.

21. 433 F. Supp. 97, 100 (M.D. Tenn.) summarily aff'd., 434 U.S. 803 (1977).

22. At Belmont Abbey College, in recent years approximately 70 percent of the students have been Roman Catholics. Id. at 874. At Pfeiffer College, approximately 40 percent of the students have been United Methodists. Id. at 876.

23. Id. at 874.

24. Id. at 876. Because of the history and character of a religiously affiliated college, recruitment of students is in many instances more fruitful among congregations familiar with the college and its ties with the church. Although this kind of recruitment will generally produce

a student body predominantly composed of members of the sponsoring religious body, the conscious design of the college may be quite simply to attract students to the campus by using an effective recruitment device.

25. Id. at 874.

26. Id. at 876.

27. See, e.g., Rev. Rul. 71-447, 1971-2 C.B. 230; Rev. Proc. 72-54, 1972-2 C.B. 834; Rev. Rul. 75-231, 1975-1 C.B. 158; and Rev. Proc. 75-50, 1975-2 C.B. 591.

28. See also Bob Jones University v. United States, 79-1 U.S.T.C. P9155 (Civ. Action No. 76-775, D.S.C., Jan. 11, 1979). But see Bob Jones University v. Johnson, 396 F. Supp. 597 (D.S.C.), aff'd., 529 F. 2d 514 (4th Cir. 1975); Goldsboro Christian Schools, Inc. v. United States, 436 F. Supp. 1314 (E.D.N.C. 1977); and Norwood v. Harrison, 413 U.S. 455 (1973).

29. See Village of Arlington Heights v. Metropolitan Housing Development Corp., 429 U.S. 252 (1977), and Washington v. Davis, 426 U.S. 229 (1976).

30. Rev. Rul. 75-231, 1975-1 C.B. 158.

31. See, e.g., Runyon v. McCrary, 427 U.S. 160, 167 (1976); and Brown v. Dade Christian Schools, 556 F. 2d 310 (5th Cir. 1977), cert. denied, 434 U.S. 1063 (1978).

32. Coit v. Green, 404 U.S. 997 (1971), aff'd. Green v. Connally, 330 F. Supp. 1150 (D.D.C. 1971); and see Green v. Kennedy, 309 F. Supp. 1127 (D.D.C. 1970), and McGlotten v. Connally, 338 F. Supp. 448 (D.D.C. 1972).

33. Letter Rulings of the IRS are available to the public under the Freedom of Information Act and are indicative of the prevailing policy within the national office of IRS at the time they are issued. But, like technical advice memoranda issued to the regional offices of IRS, they lack precedential value and cannot be cited as controlling in subsequent tax matters.

34. IRS Letter Ruling, Docket No. 774005 (Nov. 16, 1977).

35. IRS Letter Ruling, Docket No. 774007 (Nov. 16, 1977).

36. Two state court decisions involving church related colleges illustrate the need for obtaining competent counsel familiar with the common law of the local jurisdiction. In Carr v. St. John's University, 17 App. Div. 2d 632, 231 N.Y.S. 2d 410, 34 Misc. 2d 319, aff'd. mem., 12 N.Y. 2d 802, 235 N.Y.S. 2d 834, 187 N.E. 2d 18 (1962), the New York Court of Appeals affirmed the dismissal of a law suit brought by two students who were expelled from the university because they had entered into a civilly legal but canonically invalid marriage, and by two other students also dismissed from the university because they had performed the function of official witnesses at the civil ceremony. Even though the marriage was rectified canonically less than a month after the civil ceremony, the university maintained that the event had caused public scandal to the student body. The

court upheld the right of the university to dismiss a student at any time "on whatever grounds it judged advisable."

On the other hand, in Abbariao v. Hamline University School of Law, 258 N.W. 2d 108 (Minn. 1977), the Supreme Court of Minnesota required a private university to provide a student an opportunity to contest the grounds for his expulsion and to remedy his "academic difficulties." Justice Kelly noted that "courts have invoked different protections [to students] for disciplinary and academic expulsions" because "an adjudicative hearing will not determine whether a student's educational performance was unsatisfactory." 258 N.W. 2d at 112. Nevertheless, relying on a series of cases involving public universities, the court implied that the student's expulsion had resulted from "arbitrary, capricious or bad-faith actions of university officials"; and it directed the university "to treat the student fairly." Ibid.

37. See, e.g., Board of Curators of University of Missouri v. Horowitz, 435 U.S. 78 (1978).

38. Of the nonseminary respondents to our survey, 22.5 percent indicated that they still maintain a practice of compulsory chapel attendance.

39. See, e.g., Tilton v. Richardson, 403 U.S. 672, 682 (1971), Roemer v. Board of Public Works of Maryland, 426 U.S. 736, 751, 756 (1976).

40. See, e.g., Americans United for Separation of Church and State v. Bubb, 379 F. Supp. 872, 892 (D. Kan. 1974).

41. See, e.g., Anderson v. Laird, 151 U.S. App. D.C. 112, 466 F. 2d 283, cert. denied, 409 U.S. 1076 (1972); School District of Abington Township v. Schempp, 374 U.S. 203 (1963), and Engel v. Vitale, 370 U.S. 421 (1962).

42. Model Anti-Discrimination Act, section 503 (1), as printed in *Suggested State Legislation* 16 (1967), published by the Council of the State Governments (emphasis added).

43. Ohio Rev. Code 4112.02(K); Minn. Laws Ann., Sec. 363.02; Pa. Stat. Ann., Sec. 5004 (aa) (1); Consol. Laws of N.Y. Ann., Art. 15, Sec. 296.11; Ann. Laws of Mass. C 151 B (15).

44. Consol. Laws of N.Y., Book 16, Education Law, Sec. 313 (1).

45. Ibid., Sec. 313 (2) (b).

46. Ibid., Sec. 313 (3) (a).

7. Use of Publicly Funded Facilities

1. See, e.g., Clayton v. Kervick, 285 A 2d 11 (1971).

2. See Moots and Gaffney, Chapter 4, note 2 supra.

3. Ibid., variable 114.

4. P.L. 88–204, 77 Stat. 363, as amended by P.L. 89–329, P.L. 92–318, 86 Stat. 301, and P.L. 94–482, 90 Stat. 2081, 20 U.S.C. §1132 (e)–1 (B) (iii).

5. 20 U.S.C. §1163 e(c).

6. Direct Project Grant and Contract Programs, 45 CFR §100a et seq. (1977) and Financial Assistance for Construction of Higher Education Facilities, 45 CFR §170 (1977).

7. 403 U.S. at 680.

8. 426 U.S. at 756.

9. 429 F. Supp. at 875.

10. In *Tilton*, the Court invalidated the provision in the Higher Education Facilities Act which removed the interest of the government in buildings funded in part with federal assistance twenty years after the grant or commencement of a loan. In all other respects the act was sustained. For descriptions of the widely divergent and often conflicting judicial opinions which prevail with respect to the broader issue of religious displays on public property see, e.g., Anno.: "Erection, Maintenance, or Display of Religious Structures or Symbols on Public Property as Violations of Religious Freedom," 36 *ALR* 3d 1257 (1971) and Comment "The Constitutionality of Religious Displays on Public Property," 8 *Capital University Law Review* 263 (1978).

11. See, e.g., Engel v. Vitale, 370 U.S. 421, 437–44 (Douglas, J., concurring) (discussing the legitimacy of the motto "In God We Trust" on currency and coins and in the national anthem, of the prayer used at the convening of public sessions of the Supreme Court: "God save the United States and this Honorable Court," and of use of public funds for purchase of Christmas trees decorated with the words "Peace on earth, goodwill to men"); see also Allen v. Morton, 495 F. 2d 65 (D.C. Cir. 1973) (allowing nondiscriminatory use of federal parkland for celebration of religious events, including a Christmas Pageant of Peace with a nativity creche); Protestants and other Americans United for Separation of Church and State v. Watson, 407 F. 2d 1264 (D.C. Cir. 1968) (remanding for a hearing to decide whether the issuance of a commemorative Christmas postage stamp was so "religious in character and content" as to be prohibited by the Establishment Clause); Paul v. Dade County, 11 AJC, *Docket* 45 (1970), cert. denied, 397 U.S. 1065 (1970); Eugene Sand and Gravel v. City of Eugene (Ore. 1977), 20 AJC, *Docket* 67 (1977).

12. 349 A. 2d 14 (Del. 1975), cert. denied, 424 U.S. 934 (1976). Some sense of the high drama of the events which give rise to this kind of litigation emerge from the following description of the facts in *Keegan* set forth in the brief for respondents in opposition to the university's unsuccessful petition for writ of certiorari to the United States Supreme Court:

> On September 9, 1973, after repeated requests from the student residents of Christiana Towers, Father Keegan, a Roman Catholic priest of the Wilmington Diocese, celebrated Mass in a meeting room in Christiana Commons. The University notified Father Keegan that such activity was inconsistent with University policy; but Father Keegan stated that he and Father Szupper, the priest recognized by the University as chaplain for its Roman Catholic

students, intended to continue such services so long as the student residents requested. At the invitation of the student residents, Father Keegan again celebrated Mass in Christiana Commons on September 16, 1973.

On September 23, 1973, the University locked the doors to Christiana Commons, posting a notice that it was closing the building between 9:00 a.m. and 1:00 p.m. to prevent further religious activities in the residence hall. Father Szupper then led the student residents who had invited him to celebrate a Mass, in a religious worship service immediately outside the Christiana residential complex.

13. 306 F. Supp. 963 (1969).

14. Id. at 976.

15. See, e.g., Anno.: "Use of Public School Premises for Religious Purposes During Non-School Time," 79 *ALR* 2d 1148 (1961).

16. 389 A.2d 944 (N.J. 1978).

17. 68 Cal. App. 3d 1, cert. denied, 98 S. Ct. 228 (1977).

18. 389 A.2d 944 at 953, citing Southside Estates Baptist Church v. Bd. of Trustees, 115 So. 2d 697 (Fla. 1959) in which the Florida Supreme Court upheld the temporary use of public schools as a place of worship during non-school hours.

19. Id. at 957.

20. Id. at 958.

21. Ibid.

22. Id. at 959.

23. 397 U.S. 664, 669 (1970) as cited in Resnick. Id. at 959.

24. Note 17 supra.

25. Id. at 9.

26. Id. at 12–13.

27. The principle of uniform access to campus facilities was recently reaffirmed in another context in Univ. of Missouri at Columbia v. Dalton, 456 F. Supp. 985 (D. Mo. 1978). The federal court ruled that while a university had no obligation to provide one of its facilities to faculty organizations, once it did so, it was required by free speech and equal protection constitutional provisions to permit use of those facilities to groups deemed to be labor organizations which had as their goal organization of university employees, even though state law prohibited collective bargaining by university faculty members.

28. The "de minimis" application to building wear and tear was also applied by the Florida Supreme Court in Southside Estates Baptist Church v. Board of Trustees, 115 So. 2d 697 (Fla. 1959). That case illustrates as well the greatly differing attitudes about these issues. In challenging a use by church groups of local school building similar to that in Resnick, the plaintiffs apparently did not show, and the court did not require evidence about whether there were any direct expenses incurred by the school as a result of this use or any rentals paid by the church groups. It is hard to imagine the *Johnson* majority adopting that posture.

29. Tilton v. Richardson, 403 U.S. 672 at 686 (1971).

30. See, e.g., Healy v. James, 408 U.S. 169 (1972) in which, in a time of widespread campus unrest throughout the country, the denial by the president of Central Connecticut State College of recognition to students seeking to form a local chapter of Students for a Democratic Society was overturned by the U.S. Supreme Court; see also Gay Lib v. University of Missouri, 558 F. 2d 848 (8th Cir. 1977), cert. denied, 435 U.S. 981 (1978), in which the university was required to extend recognition to a group of students seeking to associate to advocate liberalization of legal restrictions against homosexuals and generate understanding and acceptance of homosexuals.

31. "The college classroom with its surrounding environs is peculiarly the 'marketplace of ideas,' and we break no new constitutional ground in reaffirming this Nation's dedication to safeguarding academic freedom. . . . Among the rights protected by the First Amendment is the right of individuals to associate to further their personal beliefs. While the freedom of association is not explicitly set out in the Amendment, it has long been held to be implicit in the freedoms of speech, assembly, and petition. [Citations omitted.] There can be no doubt that denial of official recognition, without justification, to college organizations burdens or abridges that associational right. The primary impediment to free association flowing from nonrecognition is the denial of use of campus facilities for meetings and other appropriate purposes. The practical effect of nonrecognition was demonstrated in this case when, several days after the President's decision was announced, petitioners were not allowed to hold a meeting in the campus coffee shop because they were not an approved group." Healy v. James, 408 U.S. 169, 180–81.

32. Stacy v. Williams, 306 F. Supp. 963 at 974 (1969).

33. Dean Milk Co. v. City of Madison, 340 U.S. 349 (1951).

34. Shelton v. Tucker, 364 U.S. 479 (1960); Sherbert v. Verner, 374 U.S. 398, 403 (1963).

35. Abington School District v. Schempp, 374 U.S. 203, 247 (1963).

36. See, e.g., Tribe, *American Constitutional Law*, Chapter 5, note 37 supra, pp. 826–34; Nancy H. Fink, "The Establishment Clause According to the Supreme Court: The Mysterious Eclipse of Free Exercise Values," 27 *Cath. U. L. Rev.* 207 (1978); Leo Pfeffer, "The Supremacy of Free Exercise," 61 *Georgetown L. J.* 1115 (1973).

37. Keegan, note 12 supra, at 17.

38. Johnson, note 17 supra, at 48.

39. Abington School District, note 35 supra, at 225.

40. 20 U.S.C. §1132e (b).

8. Property Relationships

1. A description of the widely publicized response of Western Maryland College to a decade of litigation which challenged the right of the college to receive public funding is set forth in *Endangered*

Service, Introduction, note 1 supra, pp. 119–21. In 1975, in settlement with plaintiffs in the *Roemer* litigation (see Chapter 3, note 20 supra) Western Maryland College divorced itself from the United Methodist Church and undertook a number of controversial steps to insure that it remained "totally neutral as to the spiritual development [in a religious sense] of its students and would not adopt, maintain or pursue any objective, policy, or plan of encouraging or discouraging such spiritual development. . . ."

2. Fisch, Introduction, note 4 supra, at p. 546; see also, Gray, "State Attorney General-Guardian of Public Charities???" 14 *Clev-Mar. L.R.* (2) 236 (1965) for a state by state analysis of legislation granting the attorney general the right to supervise charitable trusts and nonprofit corporations, and see, e.g., Paterson v. Paterson General Hospital, 235 A 2d 487, 97 N.J. Super. 514 (1967).

3. Nev. Rev. Stat. (1970) §81.340. A charitable corporation is subject to examination by the attorney general to determine "the condition of its affairs and to what extent, if at all, it may fail to comply with trusts which it has assumed or may depart from the general purpose for which it is formed."

4. Mich. Stat. Ann. (1970) §26.1200 (3). This act providing for supervision of trustees for charitable purposes does not apply to a charitable corporation organized and operated primarily as an educational institution or hospital.

5. Fisch, Introduction, note 4 supra, at p. 546.

6. Mich. Stat. Ann. (1970) §27A.3601. See also Oleksy v. Sisters of Mercy of Lansing, 74 Mich. App. 374, 253 N.W. 2d 772 (1977), in which the court held that action to enforce a charitable trust could be brought only by the attorney general and that the plaintiff, who was attempting to prevent the sale of a hospital to another hospital, did not have the authority to add the attorney general as plaintiff.

7. Olek, Chapter 2, note 3 supra, at p. 875.

8. Fisch, Introduction, note 4, supra, at p. 515.

9. Joint Comm. on Continuing Legal Education of the ALI and the ABA, *Model Non-Profit Corporation Act* (hereinafter cited as the "Model Act") (Philadelphia: American Law Institute, 1957).

10. Robert S. Pasley, "Organization and Operation of Non-Profit Corporations–Some General Considerations," 19 *Cleve. St. L. Rev.* 240 (1970). See, e.g., Ohio Revised Code, Ch. 1702–Non-Profit Corporation Law.

11. §43 (e) of the Model Act.

12. §55 of the Model Act. It might be mentioned as well that statutes in many states provide for involuntary judicial dissolution of nonprofit corporations upon a complaint of certain state officials. The complaint may be brought on any number of grounds, including abuse of authority, failure to file annual reports, and failure to use solicited funds for the purpose for which they were solicited. In addition, many states provide in their statutes for members or directors to bring a judicial action when the corporate purposes cannot be

carried out because the directors are deadlocked and the members are unable to break the deadlock, the corporate assets are being misapplied or wasted, or simply the corporation is unable to carry out its purposes. See, e.g., Ill. Stat. Annot. (Supp. 1978) 32 §163a49 and 32 §163a53.

13. Although nearly one-half of the states have statutes which provide for the assets of a dissolved corporation to be distributed to another charitable corporation which is substantially similar (Fisch, Introduction, note 4 supra, at p. 513) the courts have not ruled consistently as to whether this precludes the application of cy pres principles. See for example McDonough County Orphanage v. Burnhart, 5 Ill. 2d 230, 125 N.E. 2d 625 (1955), in which the court held that it would not apply cy pres principles; but see Metropolitan Baptist Church of Richmond, Inc. v. Younger, 48 Cal. App. 3d 850, 121 Cal. Rptr. 899 (1975), and In re Goehringer's Will, 329 N.Y.S. 2d 516, 69 Misc. 2d 145 (1972), in which the courts held that cy pres doctrine does apply in disposition of assets of a dissolved charitable corporation.

14. See, e.g., In re Goehringer's Will, note 13 supra.

15. 15 Am. Jr. 2d *Charities* §§157 et seq. (1976); *Restatement (Second) of Trusts* §399 (1959).

16. State ex rel Atty. Gen. v. Van Buren School District, 191 Ark. 1096, 87 S.W. 2d 605 (1936).

17. F. Graham Glover, "Cy Pres and the Donor's Intention," 116 *New L.J.* 3 (1966).

18. 15 Am. Jur. 2d *Charities* §§158–159 (1976); *Restatement (Second) of Trusts* §399(e) (1959).

19. Fisch, *The Cy Pres Doctrine in the United States* (New York: Matthew Bender and Company, 1950), p. 218.

20. See, e.g., Wis. Stat. Annot. §701.10 (2) (a) (1977) "In determining the alternative plan for disposition of the property, the court shall take into account current and future community needs in the general field of charity within which the original charitable purpose falls, other charitable interests of the settlor, the amount of principal and income available under the trust and other relevant factors. . . ."

21. *Restatement (Second) of Trusts* §399 (o) (1959).

22. Franklin County v. Blake, 283 Ill. 292, 119 N.E. 288 (1918); Clarke v. Armstrong, 151 Ga. 105, 106 S.E. 289 (1921); Ind. Code Ann. §23-7-1.1-33 (Burns 1972).

23. Fisch, Introduction, note 4 supra, at §§568–71.

24. Allegheny College v. National Chautauqua County Bank, 246 N.Y. 369, 159 N.E. 173 (1927); Sands v. Church of the Ascension, 181 Md. 536, 30 A. 2d 771 (1943).

25. Annapolis v. West Annapolis Fire & Improvement Co., 264 Md. 729, 288 A. 2d 151 (1972); Metropolitan Baptist Church of Richmond v. Younger, 48 Cal. App. 3d 850, 121 Cal. Rptr. 899 (1975).

26. Dunaway v. First Presbyterian Church of Wickburg, 103 Ariz. 349, 442 P. 2d 93 (1968).

27. Estate of Timko v. Oral Roberts Evangelistic Assn., 51 Mich. App. 662, 215 N.W. 2d 750 (1974).

28. Comment, "Trusts-Gifts to Charitable Corporations–Nature of Interest Created-Duties of Trustees," 26 *S. Cal. L. Rev.* 80 (1952).

29. In re Clippinger's Estate, 75 Cal. App. 2d 426, 171 P. 2d 567 (1946); Town of Cody v. Buffalo Bill Memorial Assn., 64 Wyo. 468, 196 P. 2d 369 (1948); Book Depository of the Baltimore Annual Conference v. Trustees of the Church Rooms Fund of the Methodist Episcopal Church of Baltimore, 117 Md. 86, 80 A. 50 (1912); In re Faulkner's Estate, 128 Cal. App. 2d 575, 275 P. 2d 818 (1954).

30. Fisch, Introduction, note 4 supra, at §589.

31. Id. at §588.

32. See, e.g., Wesleyan University v. Hubbard, 124 W. Va. 434, 20 S.E. 2d 677 (1942); Queen of Angels v. Younger, 66 Cal. App. 3d 359, 136 Cal. Rptr. 36 (1977).

33. See, e.g., Howard Savings Inst. v. Trustees of Amherst College, 61 N.J. Super. 119, 160 A. 2d 177 (1960), aff'd., 34 N.J. 494, 170 A. 2d 39 (1961).

34. Metropolitan Baptist Church of Richmond, Inc. v. Younger, note 13 supra.

35. See Pattillo and MacKenzie and also Parsonage, Introduction, note 6 supra.

36. This is particularly important, because conditions subsequent are generally not favored by courts and will not be recognized if any other interpretation can be imposed. Even where courts find that the documents contained such a condition, they are reluctant to find that the condition has been breached by charitable institutions. See, e.g., Harris v. Ga. Military Academy, 221 Ga. 721, 146 S.E. 2d 913 (1966).

37. It is not clear whether, under circumstances of both structural and actual control of a college by a sponsoring religious body, courts might be persuaded to apply the law of property rights as it has developed in litigation between parent church bodies and local churches. In the litigation involving a "hierarchial" as distinguished from a "congregational" church, courts have based their decisions in part on internal law and governing documents of the church in question. See, e.g., "Determination of Property Rights Between Local Church and Parent Church Body: Modern View," 52 *ALR* 3d 324 (1973); Brady v. Reiner, 198 S.E. 2d 812 (W. Va. 1973).

38. But again the role of the state attorney general must be considered, see, e.g., Queen of Angels Hospital v. Younger, note 32 supra, in which the attorney general successfully challenged the agreement between the hospital and the religious order which sponsored it to pay a compromised amount for past services rendered to the hospital by the members of the religious order.

Appendix A. The Present State of Roman Catholic Canon Law Regarding Colleges and Sponsoring Religious Bodies

1. *Communicationes* 5, 1973, 94–103.

2. *Schema Canonum Libri V De Iure Patrimoniali Ecclesiae*; an English translation, *Draft of the Canons of Book Five: The Law Regarding Church Possessions*, is available from the National Conference of Catholic Bishops.

3. Bartlett, C., *Tenure of Parochial Property in the U.S.A.*, 1926; Brown, B. F., *The Canonical Juristic Personality with Special Reference to Its Status in the U.S.A.*, 1927; Doheny, W., *Church Property: Modes of Acquisition*, 1927; Dignan, P.A., *A History of the Legal Incorporation of Catholic Church Property in the U.S.A.*, 1933; Heston, E., *The Alienation of Church Property*, 1941; Comyus, J., *Papal and Episcopal Administration of Church Property*, 1942; Sokolich, A., *Canonical Provisions for Universities and Colleges*, 1956; Donovan, T., *The Status of the Church in American Civil Law and Canon Law*, 1966; (A recent and significant study should also be mentioned: "Report of the Task Force on the Alienation of Ecclesiastical Goods," Aug. 16, 1976. It is available from the sponsoring groups: Conference of Major Superiors of Men, Leadership Conference of Women Religious, Canadian Religious Conference. "The Conveyance of Ecclesiastical Goods," by F. G. Morrisey, O.M.I., in the *Proceedings of the Canon Law Society of America*, 1976 [pp. 123–37] is a fine presentation and summary of the Report.)

4. Principia Quae Recognitionem Codicis Iuris Canonici Dirigant," *Communicationes* 1, 1969, 77–100.

5. Washington: Catholic University Press, 1968, 48 pp.

6. Harrisburg: Pennsylvania Catholic Conference, 1975, 67 pp.

7. E.g., confer J. I. O'Connor, S.J., in *Hospital Progress*, Oct., 1975, pp. 12–13.

8. *Constitution on the Church*, n. 30.

9. Ibid., n. 31.

10. Ibid., n. 33.

11. Ibid., n. 37.

12. Decree on the Apostolate of the Laity, n. 2.

13. Decree on the Ministry and Life of Priests, n. 7.

14. Decree on the Bishop's Pastoral Office, n. 28.

15. Issued in May, 1973, by the Roman Congregation for Bishops and published in English translation by the Canadian Catholic Conference in 1974.

16. The N.C.C.B. *Program of Priestly Formation*, 2d ed., 1976, nos. 7 and 219.

Appendix B. Property Relationships

1. *A College-Related Church: United Methodist Perspectives* (Nashville: National Commission on United Methodist Higher Education, 1976), pp. 11–23.

2. Throughout this paper, references to The United Methodist Church are in fact references to those agencies, boards, and conferences of the church that are responsible for the particular activity that is analyzed in the paper.

3. See, *To Give the Key of Knowledge: United Methodists and Education* (Nashville: National Commission on United Methodist Higher Education, 1976), pp. 23-31.

4. See the discussion on dissolution in Chapter 8 of this volume.

5. The Discipline requires that titles to churches and parsonages acquired by a church shall contain trust clauses similar to the following: "In trust, that said premises shall be used, kept, and maintained as a place of divine worship of the United Methodist ministry and members of The United Methodist Church; subject to the Discipline, usage, and ministerial appointments of said church as from time to time authorized and declared by the General Conference and by the Annual Conference within whose bounds the said premises are situated. This provision is solely for the benefit of the grantee, and the grantor reserves no right or interest in said property." The clause is applicable in the event a local congregation seeks to withdraw from the UMC or if the congregation ceases to exist. In general, properties held by UM colleges are not subject to trust clauses, although a North Carolina conference, for example, has placed them in property deeds of its colleges. In the case of disaffiliation of a college, it could be argued that a trust clause would be operative because it requires that the property be maintained for the benefit of the UMC.

6. In 1972 and again in 1973, two different study commissions were given the task of recommending solutions to the problems of this college, as well as two others related to the church within the episcopal area. In each instance, the commissions placed merger or some such similar arrangement as a high priority among their recommendations. As these reports reached the floor of the annual conference, they were tabled without further action. The conference was not disposed toward any solution which might destroy the historic identity of the institution's name, or its heritage.